PELICAN BOOKS

THE POPULATION
OF BRITAIN

BY EVA M. HUBBACK

(A 174)

Owing to production difficulties it ⬛ impossible to maintain large stocks of our publications, and the titles available change so rapidly that the complete catalogue is of little value as a means of knowing what books are in print. If you are not already on our mailing list and would like to know when new books or reprints are added, please send in your name and address on a post card.

Suggestions for additions are welcomed.

PELICAN BOOKS

THE POPULATION OF BRITAIN

By

EVA M. HUBBACK

PUBLISHED BY
PENGUIN BOOKS
WEST DRAYTON MIDDLESEX ENGLAND
245 FIFTH AVENUE NEW YORK U.S.A.

First published 1947

MADE AND PRINTED IN GREAT BRITAIN
FOR PENGUIN BOOKS LTD. BY HAZELL, WATSON AND VINEY, LTD.
LONDON AND AYLESBURY

DEDICATED
TO THE MEMORY OF

ELEANOR
RATHBONE

PREFACE

THIS book is not for experts and must not be judged as such, since I am in no way equipped for an expert rôle. It is an endeavour to sum up for the ordinary man and woman, in an all too brief space, the present situation with regard to population problems. It will, I hope, help to arouse an interest in this vitally important subject and serve as a preparation for the Report of the Royal Commission on Population, which it is expected will be published next year. The subject is an enormous one; it has necessarily had to be compressed into a comparatively small number of words; big issues have had to be dealt with in a few paragraphs or even in a few lines; this treatment may have led to a loss of clarity and even of accuracy. For this I hope to be forgiven.

I wish to thank the many writers on population questions from whom I have learned so much and on whose material, published or unpublished, I have drawn so freely. In particular, I would like to acknowledge my indebtedness to W. A. B. Hopkins, F. Lafitte, Dr. McCleary, R. M. Titmuss, the Reports of the Fabian Society, of Mass Observation and of P.E.P. (Political and Economic Planning). But for inaccuracies or faulty judgments I alone must take responsibility. Much help was also given in criticising typescripts or proofs by Dr. Douglas, Dr. Isaacs, Dr. McCleary, Miss Neville, Lord Simon of Wythenshawe and others.

Since one's attitude to population problems is so much a matter of opinion and of personal experience, I should be most grateful to those readers who would care to send me their views on the questions I have raised.

EVA M. HUBBACK

19, *Wellgarth Road,*
London, N.W.11.
1947

CONTENTS

9

PART IV POLICIES

INTRODUCTION

No apology is needed for a Pelican book on the problem of population. Of all the questions which face our Government and our citizens in helping to rebuild life in this country and outside it after the shattering impact of war, there is none of such fundamental importance as that of the future of our people, both as regards their numbers and their quality.

This is widely recognised by politicians and administrators, but hardly as yet by the general public. Statesmen of all parties have issued warnings; both Houses of Parliament have debated the issues; and a Royal Commission on Population is sitting to find out all that can be known on the subject and to recommend what ought to be done about the problems it presents.

Our views on population trends are bound to influence our judgment on most of the economic, social and political issues of the day. These trends are intimately bound up with such questions as the function of the family, the position of women and the welfare of children, standards of living, employment and unemployment, war and peace and international trade. Our attitudes about population questions in different parts of the Commonwealth and in other countries will, in their turn, affect our relations with the Dominions and Colonies and with the world as a whole. Population factors should be regarded as among the most important to be taken into account in planning the peace treaties.

"Thus the problem of population is all-pervading: it raises most profound issues of human life, both individual and social. It is a mental, moral and material question whose roots lie buried deep in the social structure and in the nature of man himself. . . .

It is concerned with the whole fabric of society and with every aspect of family life. Our ability to deal with it will reveal the ultimate survival value of our civilisation." *

The heart of the problem before us lies in the fact that before the war potential parents were not having enough children to ensure the replacement of their own communities in our own country, in most of the countries of North-West Europe, in the United States and in Australia and New Zealand. Our task, therefore, in this book is plain: we have to examine—if only briefly as regards this country, and still more briefly as regards others—the more important facts of the situation past and present; and we must try to estimate what is likely to happen in the future, wherein "lies the ultimate threat of a fading-out of the British people." (Statement by the Royal Commission on Population, September 1945.) These facts indeed show that, if the present situation remains as it is, we, in common with many other countries, are heading for a steady decline in the numbers of our people.

We must next enquire "Does it matter?"; and endeavour to estimate what the consequences are likely to be, and if and why we should regret the possibility of our country shrinking. If our answer is "Yes, it does matter. We believe in our British way of life and in the democratic ideals on which it is based; we want to see our country still playing an important part in the world"; if, moreover, we feel that, with all its drawbacks, life here is good and that we want as many people living in Great Britain as it can hold really comfortably; and lastly, if we believe that the small-family system does not allow for the richest kind of

* *Population and the People* (Fabian Society).

family life, we must go a step farther. We must try to find out what practical policies both the Government and public opinion should support and implement in order, first, to encourage potential parents to *desire* families larger than the average family of about two children of today; and next to remove, or at least to reduce, the many practical difficulties and financial handicaps involved in bringing up a family at the present time.

But the question is not one of quantity alone. The future happiness and greatness of our people would not be assured if we were to continue to draw as large a proportion of our children as at present from parents less well endowed than are their fellows as regards health, ability and uprightness of character. How to encourage the birth of children in homes where they will be well and wisely brought up, where they will find a warm welcome and have a hereditary endowment which will enable them to become fine men and women, is a problem which must be solved, and is an equally important part of our enquiry.

Part I

THE FACTS

Chapter 1 *

THE POPULATION OF ENGLAND
AND WALES UP TO 1939

BEFORE the war the estimated population of Great
Britain was just under 46½ millions—slightly more than
2 per cent of the inhabitants of the world. In England
and Wales it was 41½ millions. At any time changes in
the numbers of a given population are inevitably determined by two groups of facts: first, by the relation of
births to deaths; and second, by the relation of immigration to emigration. In 1939 the birth-rate in England
and Wales—the last normal year—was 14·9 per
thousand of the population, and the death-rate 12·1 per
thousand. Thus the natural increase of births over
deaths was 2·8 per thousand. With regard to migration
—of recent years a comparatively small affair—the
balance of people coming into the country over those
leaving it was 525,000 for the whole period between
1931 and 1939.

Since 1066—when the Domesday Book gave us some
idea of numbers—the population of this country has

* These first three chapters are devoted to the "political arith-
metic"—past, present and future—of the population question.
They will help those people who like to think in figures to
realise the extent of the problems concerned, and will serve as
a basis for the arguments and suggestions to be put forward
later. But there are some who find statistics and figures daunt-
ing. They are advised to miss out these chapters after page 19
and only to return to them if their interest has been aroused by
the rest of the book. If these will, in the meantime, take my
estimates as to the future of our population for granted, they
can start, with little loss to themselves, at Chapter 4.

been increasing, except for a few temporary set-backs, such as at the time of the Black Death in the fourteenth century. It is even still increasing today, although, as later pages will show, it is expected that, if pre-war rates return in a few years' time, it will begin to shrink—slowly at first, but steadily, the fall becoming cumulative as time goes on.

THE MEANING OF USEFUL TERMS

So far as possible, this book will eschew technical terms. But a few are necessary. Here are the more important:

The Birth-rate shows the number of children born every year in proportion to every thousand of the population.

The Death-rate shows the number of people who die every year in proportion to every thousand of the population. These rates, however, are bound to vary, apart from any other changes, according to the relative proportion of old to young and of men to women. In a population, for instance, where there is a larger proportion of young married people, the birth-rate would be higher than in a population equal in size with a larger proportion of people too old to have children. Thus in a street composed entirely of old-age homes the birth-rate would be nil, whereas in one consisting of a group of an equal number of young married people it would be very high. Again, where numbers of men and women are approximately equal, the proportion who can marry is necessarily greater than where there is a preponderant number of either men or women. Lastly, the death-rate is bound to be higher—other things being equal—if there is an increase in the proportion of old people.

The Net Reproduction Rate. In order, then, to estimate what is happening with regard to the future replacement of the people, a better index to measure change than the relation between the birth- and death-rates is what is known as the Net Reproduction Rate. This rate is based on the proportion of daughters, born to the women of this generation, who live to become the potential mothers of the next generation. It therefore measures the rate at which a generation would reproduce itself, provided that both the birth-rate and the death-rate remained unchanged and leaving out of account changes in migration. If, for instance, the net reproduction rate is 1, this means that the present generation of women of child-bearing age are exactly reproducing themselves. If it is more than 1, it means that the next generation of women will be larger than this one and that the population will probably increase; if it is less than 1, it means that the next generation of women will be smaller than this one and the population again, apart from migration, will decrease. In 1939 the net reproduction rate in England and Wales was just over 0·8, which showed that every hundred women of child-bearing age would between them leave behind eighty daughters. This was about 20 per cent below the level needed for replacement, so that if the birth- and death-rates remained unchanged, in the next generation the number of potential mothers would only be four-fifths of the present number. If this process were to continue for generation after generation, the population would become ever smaller and eventually would fade out. This is the ultimate danger we are up against.*

* Statisticians are now suggesting, however, that the methods of constructing the net reproduction rate hitherto accepted need to be revised. This task is being undertaken by the Royal Commission on Population. The new figures will probably show a smaller deficiency than had been reckoned; which

Unless otherwise stated the figures in this book refer to England and Wales. Scottish figures are rather differently arranged.

THE GROWTH OF THE POPULATION SINCE 1066

Relatively little is known about the size and growth of the population of England and Wales before 1801, when the first census was taken. Before that time the number of people in this country was largely guesswork. All we can say is that at the time of the Norman Conquest it was probably about 2 millions. It grew slowly, so that in 1600 it was about 5 millions. This slow rate of growth was due mainly to the fact that, although there was a high natural birth-rate and practically no emigration, there was, up to the middle of the fifteenth century, an almost equally high death-rate due to bad social conditions coupled with inadequate medical knowledge. Adam Smith's statement is often quoted to the effect that, although during the last quarter of the eighteenth century Highland women were each accustomed to having about twenty children, usually only two or three of these lived to grow up. Our knowledge of the families of the kings and queens, and the many family monuments in old churches, with their rows of little boys and girls, paint the same picture. Rarely do we hear of large surviving families. This is not surprising, since it is thought that before the Industrial Revolution about three-quarters of the children born in London died before they were 10 years old.

would mean that any future decline would take place more slowly than has been anticipated. But, quick or slow, a deficiency of even as little as 10 per cent must, if left unchecked in any given population, result ultimately in its extinction; the time to be taken would in that case, however, be considerably longer.

During the last half of the eighteenth century general prosperity grew rapidly; the introduction of the turnip family into our rotation of crops made it possible to keep cattle alive to produce fresh meat and milk in winter. Scientific discoveries, such as vaccination, and progress in medical knowledge generally greatly reduced mortality—especially infant mortality—and the death-rate began to fall considerably.

During the nineteenth century—although the birth-rate remained as high as it has probably ever been until 1871, when it reached 35 per thousand—the expanding industrial system, with its greatly increased prosperity, led to a much bigger chance of rearing a large family successfully. Improvements in housing, in sanitation, in nutrition and in medical knowledge continued; and we find, during this period, the combination of a birth-rate still high with a considerably lower death-rate.

This led to such a big increase in the population that it nearly doubled itself between 1801 and 1841, and more than doubled itself during the following sixty years. By 1900, therefore, it had reached 32 millions in England and Wales. But during the next forty years—up to 1940—the increase only consisted of another 10 millions, since, in spite of the death-rate continuing to fall from 1871, a startling change began to take place about that time in the birth-rate. It fell steadily from 35 in the seventies, until in 1933 it reached a record low level of 14·4. The consequence was that the number of babies born in 1931 to the 4,918,000 married women under 45 was less than three-quarters of the numbers in 1871, when there were only about $2\frac{1}{2}$ million married women. For an equally small number of births we have to look back to the period before 1851, when the number of married women was about 2 millions all told and the total population only about 17 millions. There was thus a fall in the average number of children per family from over 5 in the 1870's to about 2 in the 1930's—a number obviously too small for replacement purposes. The position during and after World War II is dealt with in Chapter 2.

BIRTH- AND DEATH-RATES, 1851–1938

As long as the birth-rate is higher than the death-rate there is a natural increase in the population, assuming this effect is not offset by emigration. The following table shows the birth- and death-rates per thousand of the population from 1851 to 1938. It will be noted that the birth-rate grew steadily till 1871, when it began to fall, and by 1938 was less than half what it had been in the earlier period. Suggested causes for this are given later.

The death-rate,* which had dwindled, though intermittently, since the middle of the eighteenth century, began also to fall steadily from about 1871, when it was 22·3, to 1938, when it was 11·6. These figures, however, do not fully reflect what had actually happened; for—since the proportion of deaths is highest among young children and old people, and lowest among people between 5 and 50 years of age—the death-rate (like the birth-rate) is affected, not only by changes in social conditions and medical knowledge, but also by changes in the age-distribution of the population. The increase in the proportion of old people, from 9·4 per cent of the population in 1920 to 13 per cent

---

* The losses during the first world war in Great Britain amounted to 744,000, but the fall in the birth-rate during the same period—and later owing to the deaths of so many potential fathers—represented a greater loss of unborn casualties—a loss which by the four years following the war equalled the whole of the war losses.

in 1938, meant that the death-rate had not fallen as low as it would have done had the 1920 proportions between old and young been maintained. Had this happened, the death-rate in 1938 would have been 8·5 instead of 11·6.

Table 1.— Growth of Population, Birth- and Death-rates in England and Wales, 1851–1938

YEAR	NUMBERS OF POPULATION (000's)	BIRTH-RATE	DEATH-RATE	RATE OF NATURAL INCREASE
1851	17,928	34·1	21·8	12·3
1861	20,066	34·8	21·5	13·3
1871	22,712	35·5	22·3	13·2
1881	25,974	34·1	19·7	14·4
1891	29,002	30·8	19·7	11·1
1901	32,528	28·7	17·2	11·5
1911	36,070	24·5	13·8	10·7
1921	37,887	22·8	12·4	10·4
1931	39,952	15·8	11·9	3·9
1938	41,215	15·1	11·6	3·5

EXPECTATION OF LIFE, 1881–1938

The effect of changes in the death-rate at different periods can best be realised in changes in the "expectation of life" at birth in the same periods. (The expectation of life means the average age in years to which a person is likely to live if the death-rate of the year when he was born remained unchanged.) The expectation of life for men increased from 43·7 years in 1881 to 61·8 years in 1938, and for women from 47·2 to 65·8 for the corresponding years. It serves as an admirable indication of changes in social conditions, and is everywhere higher for women than for men. This is partly because baby boys are more difficult to bring up than baby girls, and partly because men are more likely to follow dangerous pursuits than are women.

NATURAL INCREASE, 1851–1938

Owing to the fact that between 1851 and 1938 the birth-rate declined to a greater extent than the death-rate, the natural increase of the population, which is the margin between the two, fell from 13·2 in 1871 to 3·5 in 1938. This indicates the great slowing down in the rate of growth in the population during that period.

Even the rate of natural increase, however, cannot tell us very much about what is happening with regard to the replacement of any given generation by the next, as it does not take into account various other important changes. Neither can the birth-rate, since this relates births to the total population, whereas, of course, it is only women of child-bearing age who can have children. If, therefore, the proportion of women between 15 and 45 years old in the population changes, the birth-rate is bound to alter so long as the number of children produced by each woman remains the same. Since younger women are naturally more fertile than older ones, it will also change if there is a larger proportion of younger to older women within the child-bearing age-group.

We shall have a much better idea of what is happening, then, if births are related, not to the total population, but to every thousand women of child-bearing age. This gives us the *General Fertility Rate,* and shows us that whereas in 1871 1,000 women of these ages were having 154 children a year, in 1938 they were only having 62·1.

NET REPRODUCTION RATE

As was explained before, the net reproduction rate gives the most faithful indication of what is happening with regard to replacement, since it takes into account, not only the birth-rate of the mothers, but also the death-rate of the daughters; and it will be remembered that a net reproduction rate of 1 shows that the present generation of women of child-bearing age are exactly reproducing themselves. The following table shows the course of the net reproduction rate in England and Wales between 1851 and 1938. The turning point came actually in 1922, and the rate became less than 1 from that date. By 1931 it had fallen so low that women of marriageable age were failing to reproduce themselves by a sensible amount. It only reached 1 again in 1946.

Table 2.— Net Reproduction Rate in England and Wales—1851–1938 ´

YEAR	NET REPRODUCTION RATE
1851	1·3
1861	1·4
1871	1·5
1881	1·5
1891	1·4
1901	1·2
1911	1·1
1921	1·1
1931	0·8
1938	0·8

CHANGES IN AGE COMPOSITION

Although the net reproduction rate was less than 1 between 1923 and 1946, there was still some natural increase in our population, as there were so many people, both in and after the reproductive age-groups, who were born at a time when the birth-rate and the number of births per annum were both very much higher. One of the most important effects of any fall in the birth-rate

* See the reference to the revision of Net Reproduction Rates on page 19.

is the change in age distribution of the population. This can best be illustrated by the following table:

Table 3.— Age Composition of Population of Great Britain, 1881 and 1938

AGE-GROUP	1881	1938
0– 4	4,031,000	3,219,000
5–14	6,804,000	6,860,000
15–24	5,598,000	7,431,000
25–34	4,318,000	7,621,000
35–44	3,349,000	6,700,000
45–54	2,484,000	5,689,000
55–64	1,751,000	4,709,000
65 and over	1,375,000	3,979,000
TOTAL	29,710,000	46,208,000

To compare 1938 figures with a date more recent than 1881 we find that in 1911 those under 45 were 32,125,000, and those 45 and over were 8,705,000. In 1938 those under 45 were 31,836,000 and those 45 and over were 14,377,000—a 65 per cent increase.

A glance at these figures shows that in 1938 the number of schoolchildren, 6,860,000, was—even if they all lived—too few to replace the young people between 15 and 24, from whom productive workers are selected. These in their turn, being only 7,431,000, were too few to replace the group of potential parents between 25 and 34, who numbered 7,621,000. Of all women over 15, over 40 per cent had already passed the age in which they could have children. One person in four was already over 50 years old.

MARRIAGE-RATE

So far, in referring to the birth-rate, we have not distinguished between married and unmarried mothers. But since in England and Wales legitimate births in 1938 were 96 per cent of the whole, it is these which constitute the overwhelming majority of births. We must enquire, therefore, into the marriage-rate, i.e. the number of persons married per 1,000 of the population. In this country it has always been high. In 1850, 859 out of every 1,000 women were married; in 1910 the number had fallen to 818, but rose again in 1920–22 to 860, dropping in 1931 to 826, but rising to 900 in 1938. (The marriage-rate in each year is very closely related to the level of economic prosperity, so that the difference between the figures of 1931 and 1938 is due largely to the increase in prosperity after the worst years of unemployment in the early thirties.)

AGE OF MARRIAGE

Women who marry young may well be expected to have more children than those who marry late in life, partly because they have more years of possible child-bearing ahead, partly because the power to bear children is greatest for women under 25, and becomes greatly reduced near the end of the child-bearing age. Contrary to the popular impression, the average age at which women marry has dropped in recent years. It rose slightly to about 26 years old in 1911, then declined slightly to 25·5 in 1931 and to 24·6 in 1938.

THE BIRTH-RATE IN DIFFERENT SOCIAL CLASSES

Neither the birth-rate nor the death-rate is the same in all social classes. Take the birth-rate. As is common knowledge, since 1871 a high birth-rate has in this country generally gone hand-in-hand with poverty; and the birth-rate among unskilled workers was in 1938 probably about 30 per cent higher than among the richer and professional classes, who were, before the war, considerably below replacement level. Thus the poorer half of the nation's parents were producing perhaps two-thirds of the coming generation; and, in general, the size of families was inversely correlated with the income level of those in a given occupation (see Chapter 21).

This difference in the birth-rates of various social classes was most marked when voluntary family restriction first began, since it was the richer classes who first adopted the new ideas and habits. Gradually these spread to the middle classes; later to the higher ranks of the working classes and still later to the unskilled workers. This being so, it is not surprising that the difference in the rates between different social classes became less and less, and that recently the biggest fall has been among the lowest-paid workers. Can we in due course expect the present position to be reversed so that there is a direct instead of an inverse ratio between a man's income and the number of his children? I shall return to this later.

The following table illustrates tendencies up to 1931. The Royal Commission on Population will probably collect more recent and more reliable figures.

Table 4.— Birth-rates in Different Classes—England and Wales, 1911, 1921 and 1931

CLASS	BIRTHS PER THOUSAND HUSBANDS UNDER 55; WIVES UNDER 45		
	1911	1921	1931
1. Professional and Higher Business Ranks	119	98	94
2. Lower Professional and Business Ranks	132	104	90
3. Skilled Workers	153	141	120
4. Semi-skilled Workers	158	162	133
5. Unskilled Workers	213	178	153

It will be noticed that by 1921 the difference between Class 1 and the lowest two classes had narrowed, and that by 1931 Class 2 and Class 1 had changed places, Class 1 hardly changing, but all other classes showing a considerable reduction.

It is also of interest to compare the birth-rate of different occupations in 1911 and 1921, as shown in the following table:

Table 5.— Birth-rates in Different Occupations, 1911 and 1921

OCCUPATION	BIRTHS PER THOUSAND HUSBANDS UNDER 55	
	1911	1921
Hotel-keepers and Publicans	94	66
Nonconformist Clergymen	96	76
Anglican Clergymen	101	78
Authors and Journalists	104	86
Teachers	95	87
Local Authority Officials	84	88
Directors and Managers of Businesses	120	103
Commercial Travellers	125	105
Doctors	103	110
Textile Workers	125	110
Civil Servants	120	113
Bricklayers	158	118
Clerks	141	121
Farmers	141	131
Boot and Shoe Operatives	148	138
Agricultural Labourers	161	155
Policemen	153	159
Furnacemen	198	179
Coalminers	230	202
Dock Labourers	231	209

After 1921 the situation changed again. The practice of birth-control continued to spread downwards, but only reached the lower social groups mainly since that date. This tendency to reduce class differences can be seen in the following figures relating to the birth-rate among owners and miners:

Table 6.— Births per Thousand Males—1921 and 1931 *

	1921	1931
Owners and Employers	106	76
Skilled Miners	174	126
Semi-skilled Workers	200	101
Unskilled Miners	156	81

Thus in ten years the fertility of the semi-skilled declined by 50 per cent, that of the unskilled by 48 per cent, and of mine-owners and skilled workers by only 28 per cent. This is not surprising if it is remembered that during these years unemployment, which results in fewer marriages, specially affected the semi-skilled and the unskilled. At the time of writing there are no figures of a more recent date.

GENERAL DEATH-RATE IN DIFFERENT SOCIAL CLASSES, 1930–32

The following table shows the difference in 1930–32 between the death-rates in different social classes (as defined in Table 4):

Table 7.—Death-rates in Different Social Classes †

	MEN	MARRIED WOMEN	SINGLE WOMEN
Class 1	87	81	100
Class 2	94	89	64
Class 3	97	99	95
Class 4	101	103	102
Class 5	112	113	112

It is in the infant death-rate (the number of infants per thousand born who die during the first year), how-

* *The Parents' Revolt*, by R. and K. Titmuss.
† General death-rate = 100.

ever, that the greatest difference is found between the various social classes; and infant death-rates have therefore always been regarded as one of the best indications of social conditions. In 1932, in the case of infants during the first month of life, the death-rate among children of the poorest classes was 50 per cent more than among the children of the well off; in the first three months of life it was over 29 per cent more, and for the last half of the first year, when bad conditions had had more time to make themselves felt, it was nearly 50 per cent more.

REGIONAL DIFFERENCES IN DEATH-RATES

In the general death-rate as well as in the infant death-rate there are strongly marked differences between the various regions; whereas the rates in the South-East and Eastern counties were in 1937-9 only 89 per cent of the general death-rate for England and Wales, those in Northumberland and Durham, Lancashire, Cheshire and South Wales were, respectively, 115, 116 and 117 per cent of the general death-rate.

"The difference in conditions between South-East England and South Wales in 1937 was, in fact, almost as great as that in Britain between 1911 and 1939. If, before the war, conditions in Northumberland, Durham, Lancashire, Cheshire and South Wales had been as good as in the Home Counties, then these areas would have recorded in the average year not 130,000 deaths but only 100,000. In short, 30,000 people died there each year, not because of any gaps in medical knowledge, but because of local conditions." (Mark Abrams, *Condition of the British People*, 1911-45.)

There are also considerable differences in the infant death-rate between various parts of England and Wales.

When, in 1938, the general infant death-rate was 52·7,
the rural districts on the whole had a rate of 47·3.
Of the county boroughs, whereas that in Greater
London was just under 50, Sunderland, with its cold
climate and its legacy of unemployment, had one of
85, and Canterbury, on the other hand, well off and
in a sunny district, had a death-rate of only 30. It is
interesting to know that during the same time (1936–9)
Holland had reduced its infant death-rate to 37, and
New Zealand in 1938–40 to the remarkable figure of 32.
Scotland, on the other hand, still had in 1936–8 an infant
death-rate of 77.

SCOTLAND

It is interesting to compare figures in Scotland, since
both birth- and death-rates are higher there than in
England and Wales.

Table 8.— Growth of Population, Birth-, Death-, and
Net Reproduction Rates in Scotland per 1,000 of the
Population, 1851–1938

YEAR	NUMBERS OF POPULATION (000's)	BIRTH-RATE	DEATH-RATE	RATE OF NATURAL INCREASE	NET RE-PRODUCTION RATE
1851	2,889	—	—	—	1·0
1861	3,062	35·0	21·4	13·6	1·3
1871	3,360	34·6	22·2	12·4	1·3
1881	3,736	33·6	19·7	13·9	1·4
1891	4,026	30·7	19·7	11·0	1·3
1901	4,472	29·5	17·9	11·6	1·3
1911	4,761	25·9	15·2	10·7	1·1
1921	4,882	25·6	14·2	11·4	1·2
1931	4,843	19·1	13·4	5·7	0·9
1938	4,993	17·7	12·6	5·1	0·9

Chapter 2

THE WAR YEARS AND AFTER

POPULATION FIGURES, 1939–46

DURING the war various startling changes took place in both the marriage- and birth-rates, though the death-rates have remained singularly little affected. It is desirable that these should be considered apart from the pre-war figures, as it is immensely important to try to estimate whether in the future it is the war-time or the pre-war rates which are most likely to hold the field.

Table 9.— Composite Table to Illustrate Trends for 1939–46 in England and Wales

	1939	1940	1941	1942	1943	1944	1945	1946
Live Birth-rate .	14·9	14·5	14·1	15·6	16·2	17·5	16·1	19·1
Total Live Births	619,352	607,029	587,228	654,039	683,212	744,843	685,544	820,268
Births per Thousand Married Women, age 15–45 . .	108	98	94	103	107	—	—	—
Death-rate *	12·1	13·9	12·8	11·5	11·9	11·6	11·4	11·5
Total Deaths *	499,902	581,537	535,160	480,137	501,412	492,176	487,916	491,759
Net Reproduction Rate .	0·81	0·76	0·74	0·85	0·90	1·0	0·91	1·1
Infant Death-rate .	51	57	60	51	49	46	46	43
Marriage-rate .	21·3	22·5	18·7	17·8	14·1	14·3	18·7	17·9
Number of Marriages .	439,694	470,549	388,921	369,744	296,432	302,714	395,458	382,969

* During the war years only civilian deaths were included.

THE MARRIAGE-RATE

Let us start with the marriage-rate. One reason for the startling increase in the number of marriages—especially between 1933 and 1942—has already been suggested. All over the world more people marry when times are good than when times are bad. During the period of worst unemployment in the early thirties, the difficulty of getting a home together was so great that

it was not surprising that as employment became better
—thanks to the steady increase in building and to rearmament—the rate began to rise.

When the war came, the heightening of the emotional
atmosphere and the natural desire of young people to
marry when they could still be together, combined with
a period of economic prosperity unknown in their life-
time, resulted in a startling increase in the number of
marriages. At the beginning of the war an additional reason for the high marriage-rate was that the "marriageable stock" itself had risen since 1931. The bumper
crop of babies born in 1920 and 1921, when families
were re-united after the 1914–18 war, had reached marriageable age, and a larger proportion of young people
were marrying. An extra source of husbands for young
spinsters was also to be found in the large numbers of
young unmarried men in the American and Canadian
Forces.

As R. M. Titmuss points out, "from 1922 to 1932 the
marriage-rate had varied from 13·3 to 15·8; but in 1933
it began to rise, climbing slowly to 17·6 in 1938, 21·3 in
1939, and then in 1940 to the highest point ever reached,
namely 22·5. In 1941 the rate fell to 18·7, to 17·8 in
1942, 14·3 in 1943 and 14·2 in 1944," i.e. lower than at
any time since 1922. But in 1944 it started to rise again,
and reached 18·7 in 1945, and 18 in 1946.

THE BIRTH-RATE

Since 1939 there has been a marked if intermittent rise
in the birth-rate. This was probably partly due to the
increased number of marriages, and partly to the desire
felt by older married couples for a child before they
were separated. The fact that married women could not
be directed to employment if they had children under
the age of 14 may have contributed to an increased

birth-rate. But in spite of the fact that there were nearly a quarter of a million more marriages in the first three years of the war than there would have been if the moderately high marriage-rate of 1936–8 had persisted, nevertheless there were only 190,000 more births than there would have been had the average birth-rate of 1936–8 been maintained. Demobilisation has been followed by the birth-rate rising to 22·7 for the first quarter of 1947.

THE AVERAGE FAMILY

The most significant figure from the point of view of our future population is the average family size. Further light is required on any possible changes; and an investigation for the purpose is being made by the Royal Commission. Up till the last few years the average family size had remained unchanged since 1930; and— this is the important point—at a size (about 2) lower than replacement level. But the high birth-rate of recent years would suggest that it is extremely probable that it has now increased, though not yet up to replacement level.

THE DEATH-RATE

Fortunately the deaths in the armed forces in the recent war were less than half the number in the first world war. They amounted in all to about 300,000. As for the civilian death-rate, in spite of the loss of about 60,000 civilians by bombing, its satisfactory character was due in part at least to the fact that—owing to arrangements for the provision of milk and other food for mothers and babies, and to certain recent medical discoveries —there was, during these years, the lowest infant death-rate we have ever had. There was also a very satisfactory bill of health in the general population.

Chapter 3

THE FUTURE OF OUR NUMBERS

How much can we learn from the past and the present as to what is likely to happen in the future? Will the marriage-, birth- and death-rates return to their pre-war characters, or will they continue as at present? That is the crux of what we want to know.

THE FUTURE DEATH-RATE

As regards the death-rate, it is virtually certain that the further progress of medical science will result in the reduction of premature deaths, i.e. of deaths occurring before life's span has been run, particularly among infants, and among elderly people from cancer and heart disease. Better social conditions should bring about fewer still-births, fewer infant deaths (Sweden in the last few years has had only 29 per thousand), and fewer deaths of young adults from tuberculosis. But we must set against this the increasing proportion in our population of people over 60, whose death-rate is inevitably higher than that of younger people. For even though premature deaths may eventually be nearly all eliminated, death cannot be staved off for ever, and the death-rate will probably steadily rise as the proportion of old people grows.

THE FUTURE MARRIAGE-RATE

The marriage-rate is likely to begin to decline, once the effect of demobilisation and new housing accommodation has passed, because of the smaller number of young people available for marriage now as compared with the earlier years of the war; and also because of the almost equally small number of boys and girls born in the thirties who will constitute the "marriageable stock" in a few years' time. There is, therefore, bound to be an increasing decline in the number of marriages in the years ahead, leading inevitably to a lower birth-rate—unless there is an unlikely startling increase in the size of the average family.

THE FUTURE AGE AT MARRIAGE

How is the earlier average age at marriage which now prevails, and may well persist, likely to affect the small-family system? Since 73 per cent of girls who now marry at 18 have a child within three years, while only 43 per cent of those who marry at round about 24 do so, can we expect larger average families? Probably not. Early marriage is often the result of pregnancy rather than its cause. Nor can it be argued that women who marry at an older age would to any appreciable extent have had more children in the end had they married earlier. It is, of course, true that women who marry near the end of the child-bearing period cannot have time for a large family; it is also true that reproductive power is certainly greater among the younger mothers. But for all that, the number of years needed to produce the average family of three—which will be required to maintain a stationary population—or even one of four or five is not so very great. It is unlikely, therefore, that—without a change in the number of children desired—the present lower average age of marriage will *in itself* increase the birth-rate to any considerable extent, though it certainly adds to the opportunities for doing so.

THE FUTURE BIRTH-RATE

Will the upward tendency which has been going on pretty steadily since 1933—and which led in 1946 to a net reproduction rate of 1·1—be likely to be maintained? Or, as in the case of the marriage-rate, is it probably a temporary upward flicker only?

This is a vitally important question. It must again be emphasised that the high birth-rate of recent years is mostly due to the increased marriage-rate—that is to *more families instead of larger families.* Moreover, there are still many families who, owing to being separated and to lack of housing accommodation both during and after the war, have been unable, however anxious for children, to have them. Once the effects of re-uniting such families after the war, and of the provision of a sufficient number of houses have passed away, therefore, the birth-rate will probably again begin to fall.* Once again *it cannot be emphasised too strongly, if we consider the whole period since* 1930, *that the average number of children per marriage has increased only to a small extent.* It is to this figure that we must look for any signs of change of the small-family pattern, and it is still below replacement size.

May not, indeed, the average family become even smaller? In Chapter 10 it will be suggested that there is still a very large proportion of unwanted or at least unplanned conceptions. A large proportion of families of the present day seem to "leave things to chance" where the coming of children is concerned; and a large number also use ineffective contraceptive measures. We can, however, expect some improvements in the efficiency of contraceptive technique; and almost certainly will find a much more widespread use of the more efficient contraceptives already known. It may well be that in the future there will be a definite increase in the number of children wanted by a large proportion of parents—how large an increase and by how many

---

* The latest figures show this has already begun to happen.

parents we cannot tell. This might be brought about partly as a result of changes in standards of value which may encourage parents to look for happiness in family life rather than in higher standards of living, and partly as a result of Government policies to reduce some at least of the present obstructions to parenthood.

One hopeful sign is that among a small section of the professional classes there is a definite tendency to have a family—and still more to want to have a family—of four children. Future trends will obviously be affected if this tendency is maintained and spreads to other and larger sections of the population.

But the increase required in the average family for replacement purposes will have to be much greater if we reckon it, as indeed we must, not from the size of the average family as it is today, with its many unwanted conceptions, but from the size parents would *now* wish it to be if they were able to make their wishes as to the number of children desired more effective. The task of stimulating and releasing the desire for more children, therefore, though by no means an impossible one, is of an even more formidable nature than may appear at first sight. The increase will also have to be greater the later it starts, since the longer the delay, the fewer women will there be of marriageable age.

PROJECTIONS*

The future of our numbers is hidden from us, and the number of unknown factors is too great to help us even to guess with approximate accuracy. Nevertheless, we cannot avoid making as intelligent guesses as we can; since we cannot usefully plan any of the social or economic policies of the country unless we make at any rate some estimate as to what the numbers of the

* From P.E.P. Planning No. 241.

population and their distribution in age-groups are likely to be.

We must therefore make "projections," which are estimates based both on what rates have been in the past and assumptions as to what changes are likely to happen in the future. We must leave unpredictable changes out of account and remember that any projections we make are necessarily selected out of a whole range of possibilities and can, at best, only be intelligent guesswork and not prophecies.

Assumptions

In the following assumptions the changes during the war—that is to say, the effect of the high birth-rate from 1941 to 1946, and the losses due to enemy action —are disregarded. No allowance is made for migration; though for the next few years, at any rate, many thousands of young men will probably go to the Dominions. Many thousands of young women with babies, married to members of the Allied and Dominion Forces, have already joined their husbands. This will inevitably have a bad effect on the future birth-rate, unless it is compensated for by as many or more young people from other countries coming to live in Britain.

Projection I

The assumption is that birth- and death-rates remain constant at the 1939 level.

Projection II

The assumption is that the death-rate falls gradually until 1984, then remains steady; the birth-rate falls, until it produces a net reproduction rate of 0·6 in 1974, then remains constant.

Projection III

The assumption is that the death-rate remains constant at the 1939 level and the birth-rate gradually rises to a net reproduction rate of 1 in 1994.

The results of these projections can be seen in the following table:

Table 10.— Projections

PROJEC- TION NO.	YEAR										
	1939	1949	1959	1969	1979	1989	1999	2009	2019	2029	2039
I	41·55	42·15	41·83	40·39	38·44	36·07	33·54	31·26	29·16	27·11	25·20
II	41·55	42·15	41·44	39·42	36·42	32·85	28·82	24·71	20·83	17·22	14·11
III	41·55	42·15	41·83	40·39	38·79	37·08	35·51	34·41	33·73	33·27	33·09

The effects of the different assumptions only begin to vary after 1949, since all the 1949 figures are based on the 1939 rates, and give a natural increase of 1½ per cent by that year. Losses would start only after that. If the present actual high birth-rate is maintained until 1949, the decline would start a few years later.

It is Projection No. II which is the least hypothetical, since it is based on a continuation of the pre-war trends as regards the death-rate. But it is unlikely that the net reproduction rate would fall to 0·6 by 1974. The drop in total numbers would not, therefore, be so great. If we could raise the net reproduction rate permanently to 1 within a generation, leaving the death-rate as it is, we would ultimately produce a stationary population only about 3 millions less than in 1939. But if this had to wait until a generation later, there would be an ultimate loss of about 8 millions before a stationary population was reached. If, on the other hand, we succeeded both in securing a fall of the death-rate and the early attainment of a continuing net reproduction rate of 1 or more, we could look forward to a slight temporary rise in total numbers that would delay the process and result in only a small decline.

AGE DISTRIBUTION

To go back to Projection II. The shift in age distribution which would occur in 2039, if its assumptions are justified, is shown in the following table:

Table 11.— Age Distribution (Per Cent of Total Population)

AGE-GROUP	1939	1969	1999	2039
0–15	21·0	15·5	11·6	10·6
15–30	24·2	19·7	14·7	13·7
30–45	23·1	20·8	20·1	18·4
45–64	22·8	29·4	32·1	31·3
65 plus	9·0	14·6	21·5	26·0

THE NEXT TWENTY YEARS

To turn from assumptions to the facts we already know about the next twenty years:

1. The number of existing children who will be the parents of the next generation is fewer than that of their parents.

2. The birth-rate (which appears to have just passed its peak) has not for many years been big enough to produce an average family of replacement size.

3. The increasing number and proportion of elderly people is preventing a decline in the total population now, but can obviously have no effect on the birth-rate.

All this points to a population beginning to decline before the twenty years are up. What will happen thereafter depends on changes in the death-rate, the birth-rate, the marriage-rate and migration, about which we may speculate, but can know nothing.

Part II

THE CAUSES OF A DECLINING BIRTH-RATE

Chapter 4

GENERAL CAUSES OF THE FALL OF THE BIRTH-RATE SINCE 1875

The Population Falls

"In 1937 was a rumour going round
  That income-tax was soon to be six shillings in the pound;
  The cost of education every season seemed to swell,
  And to everyone's astonishment the population fell.*

"They pulled down all the houses where the children used to
     crowd
  And built delightful blocks of flats where children weren't
     allowed;
  And if father got a job there wasn't anywhere to dwell,
  But to everyone's astonishment the population fell.

"Five hundred brand-new motor-cars each morning rode the
     roads
  And flashed about like comets or sat motionless as toads;
  Whichever course they took they made the public highway
     hell,
  And to everyone's astonishment the population fell.

"The laws were very comical: to bet was voted lax,
  But your betting was the only thing that nobody would tax;
  You couldn't have a wine unless you'd sandwiches as well,
  And to Parliament's astonishment the population fell. . . .

"Abroad to show that everyone was passionate for peace,
  All children under seven joined the army or police;
  The babies studied musketry while mother filled a shell—
  And all the nations wondered why the population fell.

  (* It was, of course, the birth-rate which had been falling—
not the population; poetic licence must be allowed for.)

"The world, in short, which never was extravagantly sane,
Developed all the signs of inflammation of the brain;
The past was not encouraging, the future none could tell,
And some of us were *not* surprised the population fell."

    A. P. Herbert (Debate on Population Statistics Bill, 1937).

WHAT are the main causes for the fall of the birth-rate which started in 1875 and has resulted in the small planned family of today? Is Sir Alan Herbert right? The reduction in the average number of children per marriage from over five to about two is so large that it cannot be due in any appreciable extent to any biological change—since whether the power to produce children has or has not changed at all, there is no evidence to suggest that it has altered materially. *The reasons which account for the decline in the birth-rate must be therefore those which influence the intentions of the parents and are voluntary in character.* "From having been a forced levy, children have become a voluntary contribution." * These causes, varying as they do in character and importance, do not as a rule operate singly, and it is usually difficult even for parents themselves (and certainly for onlookers) to try to un-ravel the various strands which combine to keep a family small.

INFORMATION ON METHODS OF BIRTH-CONTROL

At first sight an easy explanation appears to lie in the fact that from about 1875 onwards birth-control became more widely known and, as it were, respectable; and thus more acceptable to many who previously were either ignorant or indifferent with regard to it. It was the spread of this knowledge, it is often suggested, which led to the reduction in the size of the average family.

          * Carr-Saunders.

From one point of view this is true. But a moment's reflection will show that some methods of birth-control have always been known to certain sections of any population, and that new propaganda with regard to these methods or the discovery of new methods would not *in themselves* have led to so great an increase in its use. It was necessary for the new ideas to fall on prepared ground. Birth-control was, in short, a *means* to enable parents to limit the number of their children to whatever total they desired, rather than a *cause* for their apparently only wanting so few.

We must therefore look behind the fact of the spread of the small planned family to its underlying causes—just as in seeking the causes for war one must look further and deeper than the manufacture of armaments. It must, of course, be recognised that the fact that the means for birth-control became more readily available and more acceptable certainly meant that more parents were prepared to practise it than if this had not been the case—just as the mere possession of armaments may tempt a nation to go to war when otherwise it might not have been able to do so.

THE UNDERLYING CAUSES—PSYCHOLOGICAL AND MATERIAL

When we try to find out the fundamental causes for the decline in the birth-rate during the last three-quarters of a century, attention must be focused on a double set of possible reasons: first and foremost, on the psychological causes which have helped to determine the wishes and ideals of parents; and secondly—though also of great importance—on the economic and material obstructions to parenthood and the practical difficulties parenthood involves. How have both these sets of causes changed during the last hundred years so as to account for the middle seventies of last century forming, as it were, a watershed—before which time the birth-rate continued to rise, and after which it began to fall steadily until the thirties of this century?

These two groups of causes naturally acted and reacted on each other. Where a child is very much wanted, practical and material discouragements to parenthood are usually disregarded. Where, on the other hand, the desire is less strong or absent, they loom very large.

THE ECONOMIC FACTOR

Let us start with the practical discouragements to parenthood, and take first the economic factor. Although it is by no means as fundamental as the psychological, I will deal with it first, since although the plea "We cannot afford another child" must always have been, to some extent, a rationalisation of other causes, it is undoubted that the economic handicap of parenthood has steadily become an increasingly important factor in determining family size.

In earlier times this handicap was not nearly so great. Before the coming of our present industrial system family income tended to some extent to keep pace with family needs. In rural life and in the towns in the pre-industrial era, every member of a family from a few years old upwards could play his part in work on the land or at the loom; and family resources, whether as regards food or money, expanded with the numbers. When, again, in the early part of the nineteenth century, the change-over to factory and urban conditions became widespread, the labour of women and children, however regrettable it was from the point of view of their health and general well-being, at least gave the appearance that family earnings increased as numbers increased. This was to some extent illusory, for in such fields as the textile industry, where the labour of women and children was much used, men's wages tended to be far lower than in others in which they alone were the wage-earners.

By 1870, however, we find the beginnings of compulsory education and the development of legislative restriction against the employment of young children. But in the labour market no account was taken of the family responsibilities of the worker, so that—for the great majority of families at all income levels—each additional child depressed the standard of living for so long as he was dependent. The age of dependency in its turn steadily increased with the constant raising of the school-leaving age and the correspondingly later entry into industry. The rising standards of child-care, of nutrition, of cleanliness, of housing and of education not only added to the cost of child nurture, but also encouraged a greater sense of parental responsibility and foresight. The majority of families realised that both parents and children would be better off from an economic point of view if families were kept small.

The effect of the economic pressure exerted by children varied from mere inconvenience and sacrifice of luxuries among the better off to penury among the very poor. It is true that the main causes of poverty between 1875 and today have been unemployment, and the death, sickness or disablement of the adult breadwinner. But within each group relative poverty has been bound to increase with the number of children; since—as Eleanor Rathbone was the first to point out —at all income levels, standards and habits of expenditure are to a great extent determined by the childless, whether married or single. The tastes and ambitions formed before marriage are not given up after, so that every additional child means a falling away from the desired mode of life.

This remained true of all sections of the community except for the very rich, whose income was far higher than could possibly be spent on personal needs, and—at the other end of the scale—for those in the "social problem" group who maintained no standards at all. But for the others, it held—whether among those who wondered whether they could afford to send a second son to Eton; or among those who doubted whether they could keep another child at a secondary school; or among those who feared another child would mean that there was not enough food, clothing and house-room to go round.

From 1875 onwards, moreover, standards of living steadily continued to rise far higher than did individual incomes. The knowledge of the ways of the better-off classes picked up from the Press, from advertisements and from films and novels, made all sections of the community aware of possibilities for the enjoyment and enrichment of life undreamt of before. These new needs and aspirations required money; but though incomes increased on an average fourfold during the nineteenth century and have increased again since, they have continually lagged behind the means to satisfy the new tastes and higher standards. Moreover—as was pointed out in the nineties of last century by Arsène Dumont—it was far easier for the individual to rise if he were unencumbered by dependents. Rudyard Kipling's phrase "He travels the fastest who travels alone" became well known in this connection. Even when parents were not particularly ambitious for themselves, the more responsible among them were invariably ambitious for their children, and wanted them to start on a higher rung of the ladder than that on which they had started themselves. And this was far easier to achieve if they had only one or two.

There were some parents, moreover, not ambitious in the worldly sense, who had a strong wish or even passion to work at some occupation, such as painting, poetry or research, for which a big material reward could not usually be expected. In such cases it was sometimes the work which was sacrificed and sometimes the family which was not produced.

Needless to say, all these same conflicts still exist today.

During the whole of the period when the birth-rate was falling, education had been the main channel for practical advancement; education which not only requires children to be kept at school as long as possible, but which also, in the case of the more able, involves technical, university or other forms of vocational training. In order to be able to provide these kinds of education the size of the family was drastically limited by ambitious parents.

SOCIAL COMPETITION

In addition to ambition for their own advancement or for that of their children, a less worthy but very widespread human weakness has always been found in the almost universal instinct of social competition—the passionate desire to keep up with one's neighbours. If the Smiths next door bought a more elegant radiogram, or a bigger car, or if Mrs. Smith had more fashionable clothes or Tommy Smith one of those all-metal scooters —so must the Brown family. The imperative call of convention and emulation could often—even usually— be responded to only at the cost of sacrificing possible children. A change in standards of value alone can substitute the creative desire for more children for standards of living often wanted, not so much for their own sake as because they have already been attained by one's neighbours.

CHANGES IN IDEAS

Of even greater importance than the changes in the standards of living between 1850 and the present day have been the changes in ideals and values. Most striking of these was the gradual weakening of custom and tradition which followed the growth of political democracy, the change-over from rural to urban life, the development of education both of children and adults, and the growth of interest in scientific matters. The influence the progress of science had on the technical processes of production, on transport and communication, on the prevention of disease and, as a result of all these, on philosophical and religious thought, was patent. The fundamentals of religion and the force of its sanctions were questioned; life came to be looked on, not as something to be passively accepted as the gift of God, but as something which man could and should plan and help to shape. The biological writings and discoveries of writers on evolution accustomed the public to discussions on the physical nature of man—and helped to remove some of the early Victorian taboos on sex questions.

To the sixties and seventies belong also the beginnings of the Women's Movement. The first stirrings of John Stuart Mill's impassioned plea for Women's Suffrage rang out in the sixties and were followed in the seventies and eighties by the beginnings of university education for women, and the development of secondary schools for girls. Women in increasing numbers began to question the traditional dominance of the male, and whether being a wife and mother was to be their only function in life.

Moreover, ever since Malthus had in 1798 demonstrated to his own satisfaction and that of his readers that overpopulation was inevitable unless checked by famine, war or moral restraint, thinking people had been uneasy about our rapid population growth. They realised, indeed, that his forebodings had not materialised in this country owing to our growing power to import foodstuffs and raw materials from abroad; but they were not so certain that this would go on. The severe economic depression in the seventies wrought havoc with the idea that progress was inevitable and emphasised existing fears.

It is not surprising, therefore, that this combination of causes—the feeling and often the actuality of poverty in relation to new standards; the turning away from traditional beliefs; the newly acquired confidence in the blessings which were to be brought about by science; the changing status of women and the beginning of scepticism as regards continued progress—led to a state of affairs in which the birth-control propaganda provided by the Bradlaugh-Besant trial of 1876 fell on ready ears, and has continued to be effective down to the present time.

Charles Bradlaugh was an early supporter of birth-control who had refused to take his place in the House of Commons when elected because—as an agnostic—he would not take the usual form of oath. Mrs. Besant, a flaming propagandist, and a marvellous orator, was one of the founders of both the Theosophical and the Fabian Societies. The righteous indignation of these two reformers was aroused at the prosecution of a certain modest bookseller for selling Knowlton's *Fruits of Philosophy*—a straightforward manual on birth-control methods. They arranged to publish the book themselves, and were prosecuted for promoting the sale of an obscene publication. In the end the prosecution broke down on a technical point. But their intentions were vindicated, and the fact that two such fine people were willing to risk imprisonment in defence of birth-control went a long way towards making the need for it known, and enabling the discussion of family limitation to be a matter in which decent people could indulge.

It was thus that the more educated and better-off classes of the community received the jolt needed to start a change in their habits; and a certain proportion began to limit their families. The idea of the small-family pattern emerged and encouraged the condemnation of the large family as imprudent, selfish and out of date. During the next seventy years the new fashion spread right down the social scale, and as it spread, the average number of children in the family declined with it. "In 1890 it meant not having more than four children, in 1910 not more than three, today it means not having more than two. The advantages enjoyed at each income level by those with families smaller than the average resulted in a continual reduction of its average size." *

Public opinion was stiffened by the activities of the Malthusian League at the end of the last century and of the Birth-control Movement since 1918. It has been felt more and more that a large family "could not be fitted into the framework of social life in which financial and social advantages were enjoyed by the relatively infertile majority whose needs decided the social pattern." *

During the twentieth century, and especially since the first world war, the increasing standardisation of manners, motives and behaviour has stereotyped the

* F. Lafitte.

small-family pattern. The much larger number of alternative objects for expenditure other than children has not been accompanied by any corresponding growth in the level of incomes. Unemployment, moreover, served to emphasise the feeling of insecurity. As Carr-Saunders put it in 1924:

"In part the reason for the small size of the family is that parents have gone on strike in protest against the neglect of their special problems. Parenthood has always involved trials and burdens; formerly, however, they were inescapable, and therefore parents were unable to force the attention of society upon them. Parents were enslaved and slaves cannot withdraw their labour. Parents are now becoming free, and they take advantage of this freedom to bring the strike weapon into play. But the effectiveness of a strike depends upon the inconvenience which the community is made to suffer. In this case the community has not been in any way incommoded as yet. In fact, the action taken by parents was welcomed; therefore the grievances of parents obtained, and still receive, little or no attention. Here the analogy fails, because the parents were not driven to return to work; they found themselves better off if they remained on strike."

Chapter 5

PSYCHOLOGICAL CAUSES TODAY
1. IN THE PARENT

"What is there in a son,
  To make a father dote, rave or run mad?
Being born, it pouts, cries and breeds teeth.
What is there yet in a son? He must be fed,
Be taught to go and speak. Aye, or yet
Why might not a man love a calf as well,
Or a fine little smooth horse colt
Should move a man as much as doth a son."
        Thomas Kyd, "The Spanish Tragedy" (1557).

MOST of the causes, both psychological and material,
which accounted for the fall in the birth-rate and the
stereotyping of the small-family pattern between 1875
and 1939 still hold good today.

I wish here to probe a little deeper into some of the
reasons for the changes in ideas and standards of living
already referred to, and also into others which have
not yet been dealt with. Here again it is necessary to
try to distinguish between those which relate to the
desires of parents—the psychological group—and those
which can be classified as *obstructions to parenthood*—
the practical and material group. But it will be obvious
that no clear-cut distinctions can be drawn. Indeed, I
despair of any really logical order, since, as I pointed
out before, obstructions appear great where desire is
weak, and vice versa.

DESIRE FOR CHILDREN

In the same way, however, as U.N.E.S.C.O. declares
that "wars begin in the minds of men," so is the kernel
of the population problem to be found in the desires
of parents. Do parents today—provided that practical

and material difficulties can be reduced—*want* a family sufficiently large to provide for the replacement of the population? Or are they—even under the most favourable circumstances—likely to be content with the present low average of about two children instead of the average of three required for replacement purposes? This is the fundamental issue.

It is common experience that parents are not willing to admit, even to themselves, that they do not want several children. Usually they put forward some such reason as "We cannot afford it" or "We should be too much tied," or "We haven't got a house," or "My wife's health is not good." But aren't these often not so much reasons as *rationalisations* of the lack of desire for more children under any circumstances? Although there are few married couples who do not want any children at all, and not many who want only one, there are probably a considerable proportion who, when they have had two—specially if these consist of a boy and a girl —do not want any more, even though there may be no reasons of finance, health or convenience to prevent their having a larger family. For them, two children give an adequate experience of parenthood. That is enough. No more are wanted. And "No children need apply here!" is the notice displayed.

Limits to the number of children parents want have probably existed at most times and in most places. If we look at people living in the different stages of history, and in different types of communities, we find that the large family has been the exception, not the rule. As has already been shown—before the nineteenth century in this country only a small proportion of those born survived, and this happens even today in countries where conditions are bad and nutrition inadequate.

Primitive communities usually controlled the number of children by infanticide, by abortion or by various restrictive taboos and customs affecting intercourse. The only important exceptions have been in agricultural communities, where labour was wanted for the land and could best be obtained from a long row of lusty sons (hence the Old Testament exhortations to be fruitful and multiply), and in warlike states where more young men were wanted for purposes of fighting.

In this country the Victorian era was the first and last period in which large surviving families were the rule—on account of the combination of a high birth-rate and a declining death-rate. In Chapter 23 it is shown that the U.S.S.R. and other countries of Eastern Europe are in a similar position today. But there is no evidence that these large Victorian families were usually wanted—at any rate by their mothers. On the contrary, many certainly were not. I have been told that my own grandmother, who had nine children in twelve years, wept every time a new baby was on the way; and she was probably not unique.

With regard to Great Britain today, it is extremely difficult to speak with any confidence of the numbers of children parents want to have. It is still more difficult to know how many children people would be prepared to have if conditions for childbearing and rearing were materially improved. Moreover, the numbers people actually have often give little indication of their real wishes: many parents find themselves unable to have as many as they want, owing to practical difficulties. Others, on the other hand, have more than they want, owing to the lack of, or failure in, methods of birth-control.

The following accounts of recent enquiries into this problem may therefore be of interest, though none of them can be regarded as even approaching scientific precision: —

(1) ENQUIRY BY THE WOMEN'S GROUP FOR PUBLIC WELFARE— 1945

A questionnaire as to the causes for the low birth-rate of today contained questions as to how many children would be wanted, firstly under present circumstances, and secondly if various reforms suggested —such as bigger family allowances, more and better houses, better arrangements for childbirth and assistance to prevent mothers being so tied—were introduced. The replies collected were mostly the result of group discussions, though sometimes they were compiled from individual answers. The total number of women consulted was about 8,000, the majority being over 35 years of age who would have had plenty of time to have produced several children. They included all social types—professional and business women, the wives and daughters of skilled and unskilled labourers and many others in between. The answers received to the questions referred to showed that—under present circumstances—a very large proportion of the groups *did not desire more than two children*. There was, however, a striking unanimity that *the women in all social classes thought the ideal number was four*.

(2) ENQUIRY BY MASS OBSERVATION ON "BRITAIN AND HER BIRTH-RATE," 1945.

About 3,000 women selected in various ways, mostly at random, were asked how many children they would like to have; and from the answers were deducted those who said they would like to have the number they already had, since this might merely be a kind of defence mechanism. It must be noticed, however, that in this case there was no indication as to whether the women were basing their replies on existing conditions or on the numbers they might like if conditions were improved. The answers were given in the following proportion:

NUMBER OF CHILDREN	WOMEN MARRIED OVER TEN YEARS	WOMEN MARRIED FIVE TO TEN YEARS	WOMEN MARRIED THREE YEARS AND UNDER
None	4	1	0
One	6	6	7
Two	48	49	61
Three	16	30	24
Over Three	26	14	8
	100	100	100
Average number of children women in this group " would like "	2·9	2·7	2·5

The conclusions arrived at by Mass Observation as a result of this enquiry are summed up as follows: ·

"Only about one woman in fifteen would like to have a one-child family. By far the most popular family size is two children, which is the number three out of five of the newly married couples would like. The proportion who would like more than three children declines rapidly down the scale of length of marriage, and only 8 per cent of those married less than five years want as many as this. The newly married are the least decided. Though they incline to want very small families more than those who have been married longer, they often say they would like 'two *or* three.' But even if we assume that half of them eventually decide on the higher number, the difference remains."

As regards the different social classes, it is interesting to note that—whereas the average number of living children of mothers with secondary education was 1·2, while the corresponding number of mothers with elementary education was 1·9, the average number women in all the different groups desired was the same—2·6.

(3) THE "NEWS CHRONICLE" GALLUP POLL, JANUARY 1939

The following answers were given to a Gallup Poll conducted by the British Institute of Public Opinion. The question asked was: "What do you consider is the ideal size for a family?" The following table shows the results:

OPINION GROUP	0	1	2	3	4	5 or more	TOTAL OF CHILDREN WANTED
Men	2	2	39	25	20	12	295
Women	3	1	35	29	20	11	295
Age 21–29	3	2	44	26	15	10	278
Age 30–40	1	2	40	25	20	12	297
Age 50 and Over	2	2	27	26	25	18	324
Higher Income	1	2	32	30	24	11	307
Medium Income	2	2	39	26	18	13	295
Lower Income	2	3	39	25	19	12	292

NUMBER OF CHILDREN WANTED — Per Cent

In this case also it is impossible to know how the different families who answered interpreted the word "ideal," as here again the question might have been taken to refer either to ideal or to present conditions. Be that as it may, it will be noticed that here also the younger groups of parents say that they would like a smaller number of children than the older groups. This suggests again that the desire for the small-family pattern has become intensified in the younger age-groups. The most interesting fact which all these enquiries elicited is that, even in 1939—when war was imminent and severe unemployment very recent—and again in 1945—when the war was actually going on—people on the whole did *want* sufficient, or nearly sufficient, children to provide for replacement, for which purpose an average family of a little under three is necessary. This can be regarded as a very hopeful sign.

THE FAMILY AS AN INSTITUTION

The desire for children is obviously closely connected with the views held with regard to the family as an institution, so that it is important to enquire whether the conception of the family has changed, and if so, in what direction. The phrase "the disintegration of the family" as one cause of a declining birth-rate seems to have become an accepted cliché used without enquiry or doubt. But is it true, and if so, what is the evidence?

It is indeed obvious that the *forms* of family life have changed; and that not only many means of livelihood, but also household processes and leisure-time interests which were previously carried on at home, are now to an increasing extent carried on outside. It is also true that the smaller family circle of recent times inevitably means a less interesting and more restricted type of family life—especially for the children themselves. But in past generations a large family—the older and younger members of which were probably separated from one another by many years—did not necessarily remain closely in contact with one another once they had become self-supporting. Few of them as a rule remained at home; most were scattered in different parts of the country or the world. Difficulties of communication and of transport involved the virtual disappearance of the more distant members. Nowadays, although a family is smaller and its members may or may not all leave the home itself, a far smaller proportion (in peace-time) leave the country. The post and telephone keep them all in touch; and rapid means of transport give an opportunity for frequent reunions. During the war it was widely recognised that it was the opportunities for leave to go home which did more than anything else to keep up the spirits of members of the Forces.

A small family enables more attention (sometimes too much) to be devoted to the individual child. The wise parent—while avoiding undue emotional dependence on the child—knows each boy or girl better than if he or she formed one of a large number, and is able, therefore, to forge the closest possible links—well able to stand the test of time. Again, the old-fashioned parent of the authoritarian type is dying out, and the modern parent tends to substitute for the older ties of obedience and habit the far stronger bonds of affection. Father is no longer only the man who stays at home on Sunday and whose contact with his children consists either of giving them indulgences not permitted by the mother, or of carrying out what is implied in her threat "I'll tell your father." He is now much more often the friendly companion whose shorter hours of work enable him to be at home during the child's waking hours in a way not open to earlier generations. As regards the mother, in many instances today a proportion of her domestic duties, such as cooking, sewing and washing, are carried on outside the home. This gives her more time and opportunity to develop ties of friendship with her children than had her own mother, and to give more attention to the child's mental and cultural as well as to his physical needs.

If we consider in its turn the relation between husband and wife, it is found that the modern husband is far less than in earlier times the dominant partner with the wife as the submissive one. To a much greater extent than before the relationship between them is one of true equality, with a far larger number of shared interests. How far this outlook has penetrated all sections of the community—anyway as far as sex relations are concerned—it is impossible to say.

The fact that divorce has increased so much of late years is often put forward as a reason for thinking that the number of unhappy marriages has also increased, and that this is one of the causes for a smaller birth-rate. It is quite impossible, however, to generalise. Nobody can possibly tell the proportion of marriages which are happy, tolerable or unhappy, respectively—either today or as compared with former times. In theory, the greater amount of companionship and understanding between the sexes which is characteristic of our own generation should promise a larger proportion of happy ones. Certainly the increase in the divorce-rate before the war did not in itself mean that a larger proportion were unhappy than in earlier years. Until the passing of the recent legislation with regard to divorce, those whose marriage was unhappy for reasons such as cruelty, when not combined with adultery, could not obtain release; and it is only within the last few years that a cheaper legal procedure has made it possible for the lower-income groups to make use of divorce at all. Previously, among the working classes, where there was marital unhappiness, there was a legal separation, in which case neither partner could remarry; or the husband just disappeared. This is still true to a great extent today, but divorce has at least become possible for and is often resorted to by poorer people. A further reason for the increase in the number of those who apply for a divorce is that there is much less of a stigma attached to it than in former years.

Needless to say, as a result both of war-time separations and hasty marriages, the number of broken marriages in the next few years is bound to be unusually large, as the divorce lists already show. War-time separations imposed an unbearable strain on many marriages of long standing; while many of the young couples who married in the war years hardly knew one another at the time and had to separate almost at once. Innumerable mistakes must have been made, and where these appear irretrievable, if the young people concerned can acquire a better assorted partner and settle down to a permanent marriage, the better for the birth-rate. Unhappily married couples do not usually want children—nor where they do can they provide for them the right kind of home life.

In general, the circumstances of the war seem to have served as a spotlight illuminating the strength rather than the weakness of family ties. Perhaps the hardships most keenly felt were not physical fear or suffering but the separations and the anxiety on behalf of distant members of the family. The unwillingness to leave the family home, even when it was bombed, the objections to being directed to work away from home, the reluctance to allow the evacuation of children, the increase in child delinquency which has occurred largely as a result of the absence of the father—all bear eloquent testimony to this. It was reassuring also to be told by more than one officer whose duty it was to censor the outgoing letters of his troops that a large proportion of married men in the units actually wrote to their wives every day and sent home often inarticulate but always affectionate weekly journals of their doings.

ARE PARENTS MORE SELFISH?

An oft-repeated criticism of the present generation is that of parental selfishness. Here again one hesitates to indict a whole generation. Former generations had not the same temptations—nor the same opportunities of interests and occupations, grave and gay—which modern life increasingly offers outside the home to those whose time and resources are not too much taken up with family cares. When my own generation was young we had no cinemas, no wireless, no dance-halls, no cocktails; only the really well off had cars. Yet it would be unfair to say that the young people of today who can and do spend their money and their time on distractions of this kind are morally any worse than their parents. They merely have these new outlets, and we had not. Moreover, there are many other claims on their time and resources which even the strictest of moralists can only regard with approval. More active citizenship, a keener desire to understand and to take part in public affairs, a larger proportion of people interested in music, art, economics or philosophy, a greater appreciation on the part of town dwellers of the delights of days or holidays in the country—none of these things can be said to represent an over-luxurious or self-indulgent attitude. But good or bad, the competition they constitute with children remains. And the clock cannot be set back!

Our problem, therefore, is to try to reconcile these new interests and values with rearing the numbers of children the nation requires. It may be necessary to remind those who may have forgotten, or who never knew, that to bring up a happy family of several children brings its own sense of achievement, and its own delights and interests far more varied and of a far more lasting and fundamental character than are the so-called pleasures of the conventional "good time."

HIGHER STANDARDS OF CHILD-CARE

As was pointed out in the last chapter, the ever-rising standards of child-care and parental responsibility mean that conscientious parents wish to, and in fact are legally compelled to, devote far more time and attention and often money to their children than in former generations. Whether it is a question of nutrition, of house-room, of clothing or of education, far more has to be done than when the rules of health and child development were largely unknown and therefore disregarded by parents and community alike. Moreover, in addition to material needs, the greater and more widespread knowledge of child psychology—however unproved some of its findings may still be—has led to a great increase in the happiness of children as a result of a more intimate understanding of their mental and moral well-being.

LACK OF KNOWLEDGE OF HOW TO BRING UP CHILDREN

Nevertheless a half-baked knowledge of child psychology is not without its dangers. Some parents—especially in the middle classes—have become so oppressed by their conceptions of the psychological surroundings which must be provided for a child that they are frightened, and decline to assume responsibility for more than a tiny family. They do not realise that several brothers and sisters can usually do more to provide a happy childhood for one another than the most conscientious adoption of the latest theories, if these result in a one- or two-child family.

To bring up several children well and happily demands a power of organisation, especially on the part of the mother, which can often only be learned by experience or example. The mother of one or two children has not had this experience, and—since today the two-child family tends to be the rule—does not have many friends who have acquired the technique. (This is especially true of the many young parents who have settled in a place new to them, and whose absorption in their own home activities has not given them a chance of making friends.) They therefore imagine that to bring up several children is a more tedious and anxious job than in fact it is. They also fail to realise that many problems inherent in bringing up one or two children are solved by the companionship of several, and by the help given in a larger family by its older members.

But whether there are one or more children, trouble often arises from the lack of knowledge of child management. Many mothers, who before they married had no experience of children and have forgotten all they may have learned at school, have spent the intervening years in office or factory. They also have little confidence in themselves and dread taking on a new responsibility. Although the health visitor and mothers' clinics are there to give what help they can when the baby arrives, this is often not enough, and maternal ignorance results in discomfort to the baby, which may turn it from a potentially contented child into a wailing, fretful little nuisance.

Still less do many young mothers know about its mental and emotional development—and this is a worse extreme than is a nodding acquaintance only with child psychology. Knowledge about this important side of child care has not kept pace with the widespread growth and understanding of its physical needs. Threats and bribery, hugs and slaps, are still often given alternately according to the state of the mother's own temper and the degree of provokingness of the child. The child is over-indulged or over-frustrated in turn, and only too often grows up tiresome and unattractive, and forms anything but an encouragement to its over-tired and irritated parents to give it a brother or sister. I do not suggest this is by any means true of all mothers. A natural love for children and much common sense enables many of them to do the job magnificently and to bring up a happy, healthy family without undue strain.

FEAR OF UNEMPLOYMENT

That the fear of unemployment ranks high among the causes for not wanting another child among the women who answered the questionnaire of the Women's Group on Public Welfare is not surprising, since one of the most potent influences which affects the birth-rate —at least over short periods of time—is whether there are or are not good prospects of employment. It will be remembered that our own reached its lowest level during the depression in the thirties. "Not like my mum" was the usual phrase among young mothers of that time who were so often warned by their own mothers not to expose themselves to the fate the latter themselves suffered when unemployment caught them with a largish family.

The young people of today who will constitute the parents of the next generation are the first for a long time who have themselves had their first experience of adult life in a period of good employment, so that they ought, therefore, to be freer from the shadow of unemployment than were their parents. For the time being, shortage of man-power has enabled the fear of unemployment to recede into the background; but later, if in the meantime Governments have not managed to establish the conditions for a high and stable level of employment, it may well recur.

INSECURITY DUE TO FEAR OF WAR

The fear of future wars is the ostensible reason given by some people for not wanting more children. They express their feeling in the familiar phrase, "I don't want to produce sons to be cannon-fodder." But up to the war this feeling was probably an important influence among only a very few of the more pacifist-minded. That in other cases it was probably a rationalisation rather than a real reason is pretty evident from the trend of the birth-rate since the first world war. This declined far more in the twenties of this century, when great hopes were still placed on the League of Nations and war seemed unlikely, than in the thirties, when war was obviously imminent, or than during the war itself, when it steadily increased. In Sweden, moreover, until the last few years, the fear of war had been completely absent for generations. But its birth-rate had, before the war, fallen lower than anywhere else in Europe— whereas when war became a real danger it had risen more than anywhere else! In Germany, again, where during the thirties war was exalted and eagerly anticipated, the birth-rate rose steadily between 1933 and 1943.

But the fact that this fear has had little real influence on the birth-rate in this country up to the present does not necessarily mean that it will not do so in the future. The bitter experience of war itself, the difficulties which are arising in the way of effective international organisation among the nations, the terrible possibilities of the atom bomb and of bacteriological warfare, may well be such that fear of war in the future will become a far more important cause for the restriction of a family than it has been in the past.

DEFEATIST ATTITUDE TOWARDS LIFE

The fear of economic insecurity or of war is obviously felt most keenly among those who temperamentally have a defeatist attitude towards life. During the war, such an attitude with regard to its progress was looked upon with contempt and—if felt—was not usually expressed or acted upon. In peace-time, however, an anxious, timorous point of view which stresses difficulties more than their possible solutions, tends to be sympathised with and therefore encouraged. It is in many quarters regarded almost as a political virtue to overstress the blemishes and inadequacies of our economic and social conditions. This is by no means universal, and the power of resilience of our people and their courage has of recent years shone out more clearly than ever. Still, it may well be that the desire for safety and comfort first will continue to increase in a population such as ours, in which the average age is continually rising—it being usually held that it is among the elderly that the lack of adventurousness is most marked and the desire for security strongest.

It is probable, moreover, that since the continuous decline in religious beliefs, the proportion of people who "feel at home in the world, assured of the purpose of life and of its ideals," * is fewer than before. This lack of faith in religion has not in many people been replaced by faith in anything else. At bottom, people desire more children only if they have faith in the life which is going to be offered to them. To find an effective substitute for "the old beliefs, old traditions, old cus-

* Dr. McCleary.

toms and old standards of conduct" * is one of the toughest problems that both education and religion in their widest sense have to solve.

It was the churches which, right through the Victorian Era, stressed the importance of family life and the need for parental self-sacrifice. All the weight of clerical influence was against birth-control. It is not surprising that in later years, as the influence of the churches became less, the habit of family limitation grew. As time went on, the Church of England considerably modified, in fact practically abandoned, its antagonism to birth-control. Today even the Church of Rome no longer opposes family restriction in itself, but only raises objections to the use of contraceptives. It is interesting, nevertheless, to note that in the enquiry into the fall of the birth-rate recently undertaken by Mass Observation, it was found that the average number of children among those whom they questioned who claimed adherence either to the Church of England or to the Church of Rome was three, whereas among those who claimed no religious affiliations it was only two.

THE INFLUENCE OF FASHION AND CUSTOM

Although family limitation began as a result of the social and economic conditions which arose about the late seventies of the last century, the many reasons for its adoption which have been outlined here were so solidly based and so persistent that the small-family fashion has now become stereotyped among all social classes except in the "social problem group," which consists of people below the normal level in their mental, physical or moral standards. The task of spreading the ways of life of the wealthier fashion-setting

* Dr. McCleary.

classes throughout the nation is nearly complete—accelerated by advertisements and films—and higher material standards are apt to usurp the money which might otherwise be spent on children. It is now taken for granted that the only sensible thing to do is to have a small family. Those who depart from this habit out of religious scruple or apathy on the one hand, or out of an unusual love of children or an unusual stock of adventurousness on the other, must be prepared to be different from their fellows—and for this unusual strength of character is often required.

Closely allied with the influence of fashion is that of social approval. Few of us are immune as regards the response we make to the attitudes of others. In the Victorian Era it was the large quiverful of children which gained, if not the envy, at least the approbation of the middle classes (though the prolific working classes were often criticised by their "betters" for their "irresponsibility"). Young people who did not do their "duty" in this respect were—among the business and professional sections—looked at askance. But now the wheel has turned full circle, and it is often the parents of more than three children who are today looked upon as either foolish or unfortunate, as the case may be. Mothers often warn their daughters against following in their own footsteps. A young friend of mine who has just had an eagerly awaited fourth child was highly indignant at the amount of undesired and unnecessary sympathy she received. Again, a group of hospital matrons recently confessed that exactly the same point of view existed in all their maternity wards—if a mother comes in for any birth after the second, she becomes an object for pity or scorn among her fellows.

Chapter 6

PSYCHOLOGICAL CAUSES TODAY
2. IN THE GENERAL PUBLIC

I HAVE suggested several psychological reasons which
are preventing parents as such from wanting larger
families. I now wish to ask why the community as a
whole has not yet regarded the population problem as
one of urgent importance. Not that these two problems
can be sharply divided. Potential parents represent
about half the adults at any one time, and their opinions
are both influenced by and influence those of the community of which they form part. But unless the community as a whole is also convinced of the need for a
higher birth-rate, it is not likely that the practical
reforms required to help parents will receive the necessary support. What, then, are the strands which make
up the complex of public opinion on population issues?

IGNORANCE OF THE FACTS

This ignorance is still widespread even now. It is
probably only a minority of thinking people in all social
classes who realise that there is a population problem
at all. For this the general public is not to blame, since
even the experts have only recognised the true situation
during the last ten or fifteen years. Keynes, in his
Economic Consequences of the Peace, published two or
three years after the first world war, feared what he
called unchaining the devil of Malthus, and expected
that the Governments of Europe would have to cope
with the problems of over- rather than of under-population. The few, such as the late Lord Passfield and Dr.
McCleary, who already before the first world war
realised the implications of the prevailing population

trends, were voices crying in the wilderness. It was only in the middle thirties that certain sociologists, such as Dr. Enid Charles, Dr. Kuczynski, Dr. Glass and Mr. Titmuss, produced books on the probable approaching population decline, the importance of which was at once realised by discerning people. But it was actually after the outbreak of this war that the subject was first raised in the House of Commons by Group-Captain Wright and Miss Eleanor Rathbone; and only just before the General Election of 1945 that statesmen, such as Mr. Winston Churchill and Mr. Herbert Morrison, referred in their speeches to the present alarming situation.

Lord Beveridge frequently drew attention to population questions in the course of his Report on Social Insurance, and gradually their implications are being forced on our "planners" at various levels. But even today, unlike in Sweden, current trends and the conception of what a birth-rate too low for replacement purposes involves are still appreciated only by a few.

The great majority, even of thinking citizens, see that not only has the birth-rate never yet been lower than the death-rate, but that since the middle thirties it has been increasing steadily and is today higher than at any time during the last twenty-six years. The ordinary man does not realise, as do the experts, that this recent flare-up may well be but a flicker due, as we have already shown, to temporary causes only. Certainly he does not realise that any probable approaching decline in the population is being retarded and masked by the existing age distribution, so that there are now—owing to the higher birth-rate of previous generations—both the abnormally high proportion of people of child-bearing age and the increasingly large proportion of elderly people to which we have already referred. It is still not generally appreciated that the proportion of people past the age at which they can have children is inevitably increasing, and that for this and other reasons already indicated the birth-rate is likely again to decline and the death-rate to rise. But what the eye does not see, the heart does not grieve for. Moreover, the future is hidden, and opinions differ widely as to what it will bring forth.

LENGTH OF TIME BEFORE POPULATION CHANGES CAN TAKE EFFECT

Even those who realise the implication of the present rates know that no great change is likely to take place in their own generation; also that little can now be done to influence the number of potential parents twenty or thirty years hence, since the great majority of these—the boys and girls of today—are already born. The main results of any population policies, therefore, even though they were initiated tomorrow, could not show any effect until the next generation. Since most of us are, not unnaturally, preoccupied with the more immediate and urgent problems of today, such as higher production at home and the prevention of hunger and renewed war abroad, we have not the interest to spare for the more distant vistas. It is only those with a more vivid imagination who realise that there are some problems affecting the future even more basic and fundamental than any concerned with the immediate present, and who may be willing to sacrifice thought or money for the sake of posterity.

PERSONAL CONSIDERATIONS

There are some who do not wish to turn their attention to population matters, since to them the discussion of any problems connected with sex is uncongenial and tied up with inhibitions or complexes—many of them subconscious. Again, often an individual's own personal situation affects his attitude. Women, to whom as a rule all family questions loom large, are generally more interested in population issues than are men. Those possessing large families themselves are more inclined to support reforms to help children, whereas those with no children, or with only a few, may fear having to help support the children of others. On the other hand, the small birth-rate of the last twenty years has produced some young parents who themselves were only children and who are desperately anxious to avoid the same fate for their own, or for others in whom they are interested. I knew of one such only child of an earlier generation who made it her ambition to have sixteen children of her own, and who lived to see this ambition realised! There must also be many parents today who, having lost only children or only sons in the wars, are indeed realising the bitter results of having had so small a family, and are impressing this on the next generation.

EFFECT OF SOCIAL DISAPPROVAL

I have already referred to the mockery or sympathy a family larger than the present low average frequently arouses today, and certain contemporary influences have emphasised this attitude. For instance, the birth-control movement, which developed in this country after the first world war, and the main object of which has been to encourage the spread of information on methods of birth-control, has inevitably preached consistently the bad effects of unrestricted births on the individual family. Only quite recently did its leaders begin to consider whether, from the point of view of the nation, the practice of birth-control might not be abused. The former somewhat irresponsible attitude is now beginning to change, and it is significant that the National Birth-Control Association has recently changed its name to the Family Planning Association, and added to its original object the phrase "To encourage the production of healthy children who are an asset to the nation, provided that their parents have the health and means to give them a reasonable chance in life." As I showed before there are signs in at any rate a small section of the professional classes that a family of three or four is now considered desirable.

GENERAL ATTITUDE TO CHILD-BEARING

The present attitude of the general body of citizens, as of most parents—arising perhaps from the still individualistic type of our society—is that whether a married couple has a family at all, and if they do so, of what size, is an entirely individual affair. It would be considered an impertinence for any outside body, and particularly the Government, to attempt to exert any influence. This attitude is very deep-seated, and not only in this country. Professor Myrdal, speaking of Sweden—a country which had devoted more time and thought to population issues than any other—goes so far as to say: "We have never thought or talked in terms of duty to the nation. Families ought to have children, not in obedience to the good of the State, but for their own private happiness. Nobody produces children for the State's sake, anyhow."

In this country, also, there is a widespread suspicion that if those in authority urge a higher birth-rate, they are doing so either because they want more cannon-fodder for future wars, or because they want a large and docile labour force. This point of view became more articulate before the recent war owing to popular criticism of both the German and Italian drives for more children—admittedly for the purposes of aggrandisement and war.

There are, however, indications quite lately that public opinion in this respect is beginning to change, and a sense of social responsibility in this connection to emerge. Even Myrdal * points out that the citizen might "fear the expiration of the people in the same way, though not to the same degree, as he fears his own death." He adds that people are inclined to argue in the following way: "After all, we in this country are striving to build up a social and cultural structure of our own, better than the one we have inherited. The task of legislative reform of public institutions, in fact of all sorts of ambitions meeting outside the individual citizen's threshold, would lose most of its urge, and indeed of its meaning, were it only a question of administering to the difficulties of a continuous shrinkage of the population."

In this country the war stimulated the sense of social responsibility, since it became far more common for the large majority of citizens to put the needs of the community, not only before their own convenience, but before life itself. It should, therefore, surely not be such a far step in peace-time for citizens to feel some responsibility for preserving the community —not by facing the risk of death, but by the creation of more life. There are already signs that the more sensitive parents of today are responding to this appeal. If this attitude spreads—and education must help it to do so—it will mean that social approval will become weighted in favour of a larger family rather than against it. No appeal of this kind is likely to persuade

* *Population—Today's Question.*

parents to have a child if they definitely do not want one. But it may become an increasingly important positive factor in the many cases in which parents are in doubt as to whether or not to start or to increase a family.

Chapter 7

CHANGES IN THE POSITION OF WOMEN

LET us examine further what is perhaps the most important of all the social changes affecting family life since 1875—to wit, the position of women, their education, their interests, and their increasing participation in matters social, occupational and recreational outside the home.

It was in the sixties of last century that secondary education first started for girls, and in the seventies that university education became open to them. In 1870 women became eligible to sit on school boards and other local authorities, and in 1886 on county councils. In 1918 they gained the first instalment of the Parliamentary vote, and in 1928 became voters on the same terms as men.

.The fact that industry ceased to be carried on in the home meant that, during working hours, a mother could no longer combine paid work with an eye on the children or the stewpot. She had to choose between one or the other. The fact, again, that families were becoming smaller, and that many domestic occupations—such as the preparation of food and the making and washing of clothes—were being transferred to an increasing extent to the factory, the canteen and the laundry, meant that many women no longer found their work in the home a whole-time occupation. This was the case especially for middle-aged women when their children had grown up. The opportunity, therefore, arose for the development among women both of various forms of recreation and social engagements outside the home, and of more serious interests—such as active membership of political parties or of women's organisations, the enjoyment of art and music and of different kinds of education and of culture. All these have increased enormously.

With growing intensity, therefore, an ever-larger proportion of wives and mothers resented being tied to a life of little but household drudgery, which resulted often in overwork and bad health. Husbands tended to feel a greater responsibility for the health and happiness of their wives than during the time when their submissiveness and complete absorption in family affairs were regarded as virtues. This regard for their health came not a moment too soon—since the misplaced heroism and patience of the working mother in regard to matters affecting her own health, the toll taken by the lack of adequate attention at child-birth and her too early return to domestic duties afterwards—all contributed to the belief that if a woman wanted to keep her health, her figure and, in some cases, her husband, she would have drastically to limit the number of her children.

THE FEMINIST MOVEMENT

The influence of the Feminist Movement, of which there were only small beginnings in the seventies and eighties of last century, but which attained to considerable importance among thinking women in the first quarter of this century, made articulate the loud protests against over-absorption in home life, and the demand for the economic independence of married women. The earliest leaders of the Feminist Movement were themselves able to carry on public work either because they were unmarried or because their own families were mostly small or non-existent. Also, coming mostly from middle-class homes, they were able to pay for domestic assistance. They resented too great an emphasis being laid on home duties, since the contention that women's place is the home was one of the chief obstacles in the way of the emancipation of women, whether political, educational or social. There was a recrudescence of this attitude before the war, when the pre-war Nazi drive for more children in Germany was accompanied by the restriction of women's share both in the labour market and in public work.

Partly as a result of this earlier feminist agitation, partly in response to the logic of events, opinion has grown ever stronger in support of women's having occupations, interests and pleasures outside the home. And there is today no doubt but that the resentment at being tied overmuch by children is one of the most potent reasons in every social class—but particularly in the middle class—for the maintenance of the small-family system. It should perhaps rank with the financial factor itself, and in better-off homes is of even greater importance. It took second place in the answers as to the causes of small families in the enquiry of the Women's Group for Public Welfare already referred to. It accounts for the support given to the provision of reforms such as labour-saving devices in the home, more nurseries and nursery schools and more domestic assistance, which will be described in later chapters.

PAID WORK FOR WOMEN

To what extent has the paid work of married women outside the home affected the birth-rate?

Take first the case of women in industry. The change-over of industry from the home to the factory, begun at the time of the Industrial Revolution, has already been referred to. It meant that a proportion of married indeed, unendurable conditions. Equally bad conditions women became factory workers, under notorious and, obtained in agricultural work. It is not surprising, then, that with the greater prosperity of the working classes from 1860 onwards, it became generally regarded as undesirable and unnecessary for women of the industrial classes to return to work, whether in field or factory, after marriage. It was a matter of self-respect for the husband that he should support his family adequately without his wife's having to work.

The textile industry was, and is, a notable exception —since women who had worked at spinning and weaving in their own homes had followed the spinning-wheel and the loom into the factory. As regards other industries, however, married women usually only continued their employment, or added to their incomes by casual domestic employment such as charring or office-cleaning when they were forced to do so by the low wages, or the death or disablement, of their husbands. Before the war, then, it is not surprising that only 13 per cent of married women of all ages were employed in industry. We do not know how many of these had dependent children. During the war, when all possible moral pressure was brought to bear on women, with or without children, to undertake work of national importance, and when a large proportion of Service wives responded—largely on account of the need to supplement the small allowances for dependants which were paid during the early years of the war—only a few of those with children under 14 took paid work (including part-time work. Sixty-one per cent of married women without dependent children, on the other hand, were engaged in war work, most of whom, of course, had been directed.

Those married women in the higher income groups who work outside their homes are chiefly occupied in the professions and in commerce. An increasingly large number of women during the last few decades have been employed in central and local government services, in teaching, medicine, nursing and office work of all kinds, and a few are employed in the arts and in law.

How many of these stay on after marriage? Probably also only a small proportion. A marriage ban was formerly imposed in the Civil Service and by most local authorities. This was removed in the case of the Civil Service in 1946, and in the case of teachers by the Education Act of 1944. Where a legal ban does not obtain, the fiats of employers, custom, and, above all, the desire of women themselves led to most of them leaving their employment on marriage. For it must be remembered that an overwhelming proportion of ordinary everyday women by no means find their paid work of absorbing interest. Most of them regard it as a "meantime" occupation between school and marriage. It is a husband and a home and children to which both instinct and tradition direct their wishes. This attitude towards work on the part of women themselves is reflected in that of their employers and parents, and accounts for the fact that comparatively few among them are trained for the more responsible and more interesting jobs. Women are to a great extent still the Cinderellas of their occupations, and to them the idea of marriage is an escape from drudgery and often from loneliness—not a prison—whatever may prove to be the case afterwards!

This largely explains why, in paid occupations, the number of married women with children was small before the war. And all the portents are that it will remain small now peace has returned. I often discussed the question of paid work for married women with many groups of young women in the Forces. I do not think that I ever met *one* woman among the whole lot who liked to contemplate the idea of returning to any sort of paid work after marriage. Earning the family income was, they said, the husband's affair—their own economic independence did not seem to them of any importance. It is not likely, therefore, unless their point of view changes very much, that employment of married women, still less of mothers, in paid occupations will increase to any appreciable extent. Only a small proportion of married women have remained in industry since the war in spite of urgent Government appeals.

There are, however, two exceptional groups. One is still the cotton industry; and it is significant that, with its long-established tradition of retaining women employees after marriage, this had in 1932 a fertility-rate of 110 per thousand married women, whereas in the mining industry, which was carried on in areas where there was no employment for married women, the comparable figure was 202. It cannot be doubted that the wider choice of occupations alternative to child-bearing was largely responsible for this difference.

The second exception is to be found among women in the more interesting professions, such as teaching, medicine, the arts and the higher administrative positions in Government service or in industry. These women have spent long years in training, are interested in their jobs, and often very loth to give them up after marriage. Since under present conditions, at any rate, the pursuit of a career has usually been found incompatible with any but a small family, the desire on the part of the professional woman to stay at work is apt to be at the expense of the numbers of her children. The numbers of professional women of this kind may not be great, but they tend to belong to the fashion-setting class and may well influence others in the same direction in whose case the question of professional duties may not arise. It is also the professional women who are the most articulate, which accounts for the probability that the desire to enter or retain paid work on the part of ordinary mothers is much less than is often represented.

Chapter 8

SOME PRACTICAL OBSTRUCTIONS TO PARENTHOOD

(1) HOUSING DIFFICULTIES

FOR some time past one of the most acute problems involved in having a family has been the shortage of suitable accommodation. Although just before the war the people of this country were better housed than they had ever been, in this case again their standards of what was desirable had risen more than the actual achievements. The best of the houses built between the wars had set a new standard, though even in these the usual three bedrooms (one of which was very small) did not provide enough space for families with more than three children.

In spite, then, of the $4\frac{1}{2}$ million houses built between the two wars, there were still left in 1939 7 millions built before 1914—many of them very much before. A large proportion of these were, from a family point of view, unsuitable to the last degree. Slums were still in existence all over the country, where houses and tenements alike lacked all the amenities of civilised existence. The big blocks of flats, which were put up in London and a few other big towns to replace small slum dwellings, were thoroughly unsuitable for children and provided few gardens or places in which to play. Children could often not be brought up in these without injury to their own development or overwork on the part of the mother. In one such block, for instance, I quite recently saw a woman dragging a pram up five flights of stone stairs!

The unplanned growth of large towns, the frequent inadequacy of open spaces, the increasing toll of the roads, the long distances from the open country—all serve to produce a pattern of life into which children do not fit. Even the comparatively few larger houses which were built or were already in existence before the war were only too often not available for the larger family, since both the rents and rates were too high for poor parents to pay, in addition to supplying the children's other needs. A famous enquiry made at Stockton-on-Tees some years before the war showed that children removed from a slum area to a new housing estate had definitely deteriorated in health on account of the fact that the enforced additional expenditure in rent had had to be made at the cost of expenditure on food. In spite of the 1930 Housing and Slum Clearance Act having empowered local authorities to give their housing subsidies—or part of them—in the form of children's rent rebates, only about 112 of these authorities in Great Britain had, before the war, adopted this system. The majority used instead the flat-rate subsidy, which reduced rents for all alike. The fact, moreover, that rates are based on rent, and therefore increase with the rent of the house, is a direct contradiction of the principle that taxation should be in accordance with ability to pay, and adds to the difficulties of housing adequately a larger family.

The Present Situation

As a result partly of the hold-up of building during the war and of the destruction by bombing, and partly of the large additional number of marriages and consequent increase in the number of families, very many families today have no homes of their own. This is particularly true of young married people, of whom a large proportion are sharing with relatives and friends or are in furnished rooms. It is not surprising that these are not tempted to start or to increase a family. It is notorious that the ordinary landlord, unconcerned, as are most other citizens, with the population problem, does all he can to avoid letting his house to families with children. He knows only that children are destructive and noisy, and "no encumbrances" has become so usual a condition that the parents of even a small family have often an almost impossible problem of accommodation to solve.

As a result of all these difficulties, the housing shortage has today priority over all our social post-war problems, and it is those with children whose needs are the most acute. 361 groups out of the 450 who took part in the enquiry instituted by the Women's Group on Public Welfare into the causes for the small family, already mentioned, placed housing difficulties first in importance among these causes.

The temporary houses now being provided by local housing authorities are admittedly only large enough to take two young children, and there is as yet no assurance that the permanent houses to be built are going to include among them enough large houses for anything like the number of bigger families the population situation requires; or that if they do, the rents will be within the reach of the family man. It is not a happy augury that, as regards the new subsidies provided by the State and local housing authorities, there is no differentiation proposed for houses of different sizes up to three bedrooms, and no subsidies at all payable on houses with more than three bedrooms.

(2) EDUCATIONAL DIFFICULTIES
Expenses of Education

Up to the present the cost of education has always been one of the reasons most often given by the more responsible types of parents for restricting their family to one or two. This tendency, it was pointed out in Chapter 4, had become more marked during the last quarter of the nineteenth century, when efficiency in examinations was gradually substituted for privilege and patronage as a means of entering the learned professions and the Civil Service; and when the need for greater technical efficiency made it imperative that more responsible working-class parents should give their children the opportunity of attending technical schools or of being apprenticed to a skilled trade.

Few children grow up in this country without some form of parental sacrifice for educational purposes. Even where the State has borne the burden of the cost of education, as it has increasingly done, the delayed entry into a job which the continual raising of the school-leaving age has involved has increased correspondingly the length of the period of child dependency. In particular, to keep a child on at school past the minimum school-leaving age has always meant a loss of the child's potential earnings. Of late years the dwindling birth-rate has put a premium on the juvenile worker which has led to a considerable increase in his or her earning powers. A skilled girl typist 16 years old, for instance, today earns between £150 and £200 a year; against this—if she remains at school—only a very small sum for maintenance allowances can be set.

The richer business and professional classes, as is widely publicised, usually send their boys—and to an increasing extent their girls—to independent and expensive boarding schools, preparatory or public. Those with somewhat lower incomes send them as a rule to independent or "direct grant" day schools, which before the 1944 Act had fees considerably higher than in schools maintained or aided by the local authority.

These high fees are still paid often by those to whom it entails considerable financial sacrifice because of the advantages both educational and social (many of which are very real) that these schools appear to the parents to offer.

Take, for instance, the public schools—whether boys' or girls'. Many of these are richly endowed and have their own individual traditions, a relatively large and well-paid staff, good buildings, playing-fields, and, in the case of boarding schools, opportunities for life in the country. More than this, the boys' public schools at any rate give scholarships to enable a comparatively large proportion of their pupils to go on to a university, and thus to qualify for many higher business and professional posts. Even for those who do not thus go on the old school tie still serves as an open sesame to many posts and occupations.

There are also, at the other extreme, a number of small independent schools, often inefficient and housed in unsuitable buildings, for which parents have been prepared to pay, either because they prefer a small school or because they wish their children to have the companionship of other children from the same social class as their own. Under the new Education Act these schools will be permitted to exist only when up to a certain standard, which will considerably increase the expense of running them and therefore their fees.

In the rate-aided schools, about half the children were fee-payers before the 1944 Act. The fees in these schools amounted to from £4 to £12 per term, and, whether fees were charged or not, there were additional expenses amounting to perhaps £3 during the term. These fees and expenses have certainly acted as a deterrent to an increasing birth-rate.

As regards numbers the children in "public" schools

are rather less than 2 per cent of their age-group; and those in State-aided grammar schools only about 16 per cent. So it may be argued that the "public-schools" group of families have had only a negligible effect on the birth-rate, and those whose children attend a grammar school a not very important one—however much they restrict the number of their children. But it must be remembered that both these categories come from the fashion-setting classes and that their unconscious influence has affected far larger circles than their own.

With regard to demands, other than fees, made on parents of children in the primary and other non-fee-paying schools, they are far greater now than in the past because of the rise in the standard of child-care. Better nutrition, better clothing, greater cleanliness, better health, greater medical care than in former times are required from all parents. The response, except among the subnormal parents, keeps pace with the demand. The children of today are healthier, larger, better fed, shod and clothed than they have ever been before. But undoubtedly this improvement of quality has been at the expense of their quantity. Can we hope that in the future this will not be so?

The Future

The great 1944 Education Act aims at carrying out the principle of equality of opportunity. It embodies the view "that the child is the centre of education, and that so far as possible all children should receive the type of education for which they are best adapted." For this purpose, from April 1945, free secondary education was provided at all schools maintained or aided by a local authority; and also at many of those previously receiving direct Ministry of Education grants.

It is hoped that, as soon as is practicable, reforms will be introduced which will make all State-aided schools so good that there will be no temptation for parents to indulge in expensive forms of private education. We shall be referring in a later chapter to what is necessary for this purpose. Today, however, Utopia is still far away, and it will take a very long time before the size of classes, the standards of building and playing-fields will be as good in the State as in the best types of independent schools. Those schools which elect to remain independent, therefore, will have to charge even higher fees than they have done so far in order to pay for the ever-increasing expenses of education; and—where they have been in receipt of grants from the Ministry of Education—to compensate for the withdrawal of the grants, which is the penalty involved by retaining their independence. Parents who wish to send their children to such schools, therefore, may well feel bound to restrict their families more than ever.

The Education Act, indeed, may in itself provide a new reason for parents wishing to send their children to independent schools, since in the future it will be the local education authority who in the main will determine to which type of secondary school—grammar, technical or modern—a child must be sent. This will often fail to fit in with the wishes of the parents, who in so many cases prefer a grammar school because of the black-coated occupations to which it leads. These may then take refuge—if they can possibly afford it—in sending their child to an independent school. This might be less likely to happen if and when multilateral secondary schools are established at which all types of secondary education can be provided at the same school —but I doubt it! On the other hand, there will be certain categories of parents previously fee-paying who when the fees are raised will give up the struggle and, however unwillingly, send their children to the non-fee-paying schools. No one can say whether the former or latter of these groups of parents will be the larger.

Higher Education

It is not, however, only school education on which a proportion of ambitious parents are prepared to spend money, and on account of which they may keep down the numbers of their children. For to enter the best and most interesting careers of all—the learned professions, and increasingly the higher ranges of business—it is the university or other forms of higher education, such as full-time technical institutions, which are essential. In fact, for many occupations such as medicine, law, and the highest forms of engineering, both university and post-university training are sometimes necessary and nearly always desirable.

The number of university scholarships and bursaries is by no means large enough to ensure that the limited number of university student places (in Great Britain there are about 75,000) are selected according to ability of the students rather than to the purses of the parents. It is true that in Oxford and Cambridge over half of the students have scholarships or bursaries to help them with their fees. But only a small proportion of these cover the whole expenses of the student all the year round, and in other universities scholarships are very few and far between.

Fortunately the Education Act of 1944 provides for an increase in the number and amount of State university scholarships. Many ex-service men and women, prospective teachers and others already have their training free, and the recent Goodenough Report on training for the medical profession recommends free training for all medical students. It has been estimated, however, that the number of university students in this country could be multiplied five times without reducing to any appreciable extent the standard of university work. This indicates the vast amount of intellectual ability that is not being trained up to its maximum potentiality, either for lack of means or for lack of university places, and emphasises the need for more free university and post-university training.

(3) THE HEALTH OF THE MOTHER

Fear of Childbirth and Pregnancy

In spite of the increasingly low records in the number of deaths in childbirth, and in spite of the great improvement in the health of mothers before and after childbirth—due largely to the fine work of ante- and post-natal clinics—a small proportion of women (or their husbands on their behalf) are undoubtedly influenced against having another child by their fears. It may be that the very campaign which so successfully aimed at reducing the comparatively high maternal death-rate of former years, by stressing the unnecessary deaths in itself caused alarm among certain women. The numbers of those affected by these fears, however, must not be exaggerated. Most of the groups of women who took part in the enquiry by the Women's Group for Public Welfare placed the fear of childbirth very low among the causes for the small family—only twelve giving it one of the first four places (as against 140 who placed bad housing first), and 102 placing it last of all. In the Mass Observation enquiry, the same conclusion was reached. But both these investigations agree that, although not of numerical importance, it is a very potent reason both among the exceptionally nervous and among the few who have either suffered themselves to an unusual extent at or after childbirth, or whose friends have had particularly difficult or dangerous times. It should be noted, moreover, that much indignation has rightly been aroused among working-class women at the anæsthetics habitually used by doctors for their better-off sisters not being usually available for those attended by midwives. Recently, however, midwives have been allowed to use certain kinds of anæsthetics, though few are yet qualified to do so.

Pregnancy

The prospect of another nine months of pregnancy is, however, a deterrent far more often than is fear of the confinement itself. Discomfort, at least, is very frequent —especially among those who live in bad conditions and are not well fed, and who can get no assistance with the care of the house and existing children. And it is not only the discomforts a woman—especially a young woman—worries about. It is perhaps more often the effect on her appearance, and the fact that she will not be able to go about as usual with her husband. In the less happy marriages, moreover, she sometimes fears a strain on her husband's faithfulness.

Bad Health and Fertility

There is a good deal of evidence to show that the level of health in this country among the masses of the people is not nearly as good as it should be. This is not surprising, as up to the present there have been many gaps and inadequacies in our health services. Medical inspection of schoolchildren only started in 1909, so that the older parents today were mostly without medical care in their youth. Even now the School Medical Services are very perfunctory. It is not possible to examine twenty or more children in an hour and really find out what is wrong as regards anything not quite obvious. The machinery for treatment and for bringing pressure to bear on neglectful parents to carry out that treatment is also still defective. This is even more true of dental treatment, so that as a nation the state of our teeth leads to much preventable ill-health.

The National Health Insurance system, in its death-throes at the time of writing, has in its turn been full of gaps and inadequacies. The number of persons per panel doctor is too high, the treatment permitted too limited, and the treatment actually given more limited still. Worst of all, it is only available for insured persons, so that children under working age, and all women except those engaged in paid work, have been outside its scope.

The result is that in the poorer sections of the working classes, home-keeping mothers and their children have had very little medical attention, as they have been denied the benefits of national insurance and often have not been able to afford a family doctor. As for married working women who are engaged in paid work, the National Health Insurance figures show that so high has the sickness rate been among them, that some years ago their sickness benefit was actually lowered on account of the high number of claims. Only too many mothers who have had several children take it as a matter of course that they suffer from debility, backache and indigestion and never really feel well. This largely arises both from inadequate care after childbirth, and a too early return to household duties, and from bad conditions as regards nutrition and housing.

Some astonishing figures were given by the Peckham Health Centre, whose doctors take a very gloomy view with regard to the standard of health of the average working-class family. In the five years immediately preceding the outbreak of war, for instance, they conducted periodic health overhauls of 1,206 families. Of the 3,911 individuals of both sexes and all ages which these families represented, they considered 90 per cent had one or more pathological disorders. They found that only 14 per cent of the men and boys and 4 per cent of the women and girls had nothing wrong. While over two-thirds of those concerned did not feel that their health was below standard, add the writers of the report, this did not mean that it had no effect on their lives. On the contrary, it involved a sapping of "the individual's spontaneous courage for adventure and zest for living." It is to this the authors of the Peckham Experiment attribute "a high percentage of infertility, of non-consummation of marriage, of rarity of connection, as well as a deliberate avoidance of child-bearing by birth-control methods."

It is only fair to add that other doctors by no means share this view that ill-health is so general; but it may well be true of a considerable section of the population.

Chapter 9

INVOLUNTARY CHILDLESSNESS

THERE are, and of course always have been, a certain
proportion of people who are physically unable either
to have any children at all or to have as many as they
wish. It is important to try to find out the extent of involuntary childlessness, and whether it is increasing or
decreasing. It is also necessary to enquire into the
causes of sterility in order to see what remedies may be
found.

Different individuals vary with regard to their inherent capacity for reproduction, their sex habits and
their liability to involuntary miscarriages and to
still-births. Some of the factors which influence the
power to have children depend on hereditary make-up,
and some, such as the quantity and quality of food or
of medical services, on environment. All these must be
taken into account in trying to solve the problem.

CHILDLESSNESS IN 1911 AND TODAY

Since the 1911 Census, no statistics have been kept
in England and Wales of the proportion of childless
marriages. It is therefore impossible to say whether
and in what direction these have varied. The facts as
to the proportion of childless marriages and the distribution of children in different families today are being
investigated by the Royal Commission on Population,
and their conclusions will be published soon after this
book appears. In 1911 Professor Kuczynski stated "of
the women in England and Wales who concluded their
marriage before the age of 25 and who had been married for over ten years, the proportion who had not
had a live child born of their present marriage was
5·2. Of those who had married before the age of 20

the proportion was 3·2." Thus in 1911 over 94 per cent of all marriages resulted in children. A certain number of even this small proportion of childless marriages were of course due to parents' not wishing to have children. But in any case involuntary childlessness cannot be regarded as anything but an unimportant cause of the 39 per cent decline in the gross reproduction rate up to the war. There seems to be indeed nothing to suggest that since 1911 unwanted sterility has increased; and as, during the last thirty years, much more medical knowledge has been gained as to the means of combating both physiological and psychological causes of childlessness, it is probable that many married couples who would not have been able to have children in earlier periods are able to do so today.

Recent investigations, however, with regard to groups of women in different social classes who have been married for at least five years have shown that, in about 90 per cent of the cases of childless couples, the absence of children is not caused by their own desire. In an enquiry undertaken in 1944 by Mass Observation, out of sixty-six women who had not had a child after five or more years of marriage, only four confessed to having never wanted children at all, and only seventeen appear to have deliberately avoided having any. Of the forty-nine wives who would have liked children, twenty-five said they were unable to conceive and thirteen gave as reasons still-births, miscarriages and the bad health either of themselves or of their husbands. This is a tiny sample, but is possibly indicative of the situation.

CAUSES OF STERILITY

Among the causes why potential parents, though wanting children, are not in fact able in some cases to conceive them, or in others to bring them through the various risks of pregnancy and childbirth, are the following:

(1) *Physical Causes*

Sterility may be due to malformations, obstructions, impotence or other physical troubles in the reproductive organs of either men or women, to infertility of the male sperm, or to miscarriages and still-births. The increase of medical knowledge has enabled these troubles to be more often successfully tackled, but they are still serious.

(2) *Malnutrition*

The deprivation of the right kind of food for expectant mothers leads sometimes both to infertility and to an increased proportion of miscarriages and still-births. But much more is now known than in former times about nutrition; and in general the food values, protective and otherwise, contained in the diet of the great majority of people in this country, have improved remarkably since 1875, when the birth-rate began to decrease. It is unlikely, therefore, that there has been any increase in sterility on this account.

(3) *Mental Strain*

Nervous stress and strain, it is sometimes alleged, tends to produce infertility. While there are certain indications, such as the increase of neurasthenia and mental breakdowns, which suggest that the stress of living today may be greater than formerly—especially in war-time—it is probable that any effect on the reproductive capacity that this may have had has been offset, or more than offset, by improvements in food and other physical conditions already referred to. Some believe, moreover, that for many sections of the community and in many ways life is *less* difficult than in earlier times. There is certainly much less grinding poverty.

(4) *Marital Maladjustment*

In many cases no reason can be found to account for a couple who want children not being able to have any; sometimes this may be due to maladjustments, whether psychological or physical, conscious or sub-conscious, between the two partners, each of whom might have been able to have a child by another spouse.

(5) *Innate Reproductive Capacity*

It is sometimes suggested that innate reproductive capacity may have declined. On this it is impossible for a layman to give an opinion, although one might have expected it to improve, since inevitably the least fecund strains tend to die out. But in any case, no change of this kind is likely to have been sudden; and probably could show its effects only after many genera-tions had passed—far more than since 1875, when the decline in our birth-rate first set in.

RELATIVE CHILDLESSNESS

What is even more difficult to estimate than the amount of total childlessness is the number of parents who, while they have had one or two children success-fully, find themselves physically unable to have more when they wish to. This relative sterility is prob-ably much more frequent than total sterility. As in the childless marriage, it may be due to such causes as low reproductive capacity or to psychological or physical difficulties which render conception unlikely. But it may also be due to injuries caused at the birth of the first child, to the fear of repetition of a difficult birth, or to the fact that all conceptions after the first have resulted in miscarriages, still-births or infant deaths.

Chapter 10

FAMILY LIMITATION AND THE UNWANTED CONCEPTION

THE heading to this chapter does not say "unwanted children," because of these, fortunately, there are probably very few. However much a child may have been unplanned for, or even unwanted before he is born, by the time he arrives he is generally welcome. This attitude is familiarly expressed as "you wouldn't be without them once you've got them!" But it is common knowledge that a very large proportion of conceptions in any social class are uninvited—anyhow, at the time they occur.

I know of only two enquiries in this country into the matter, both very small. At the Peckham Health Centre, records were kept during 1943 of sixty-two babies conceived after their parents had joined the Centre. Of these conceptions, six were actively resented, twenty-six were accidental, thirty were deliberate. That is to say, more than half of them would presumably not have taken place had the parents been able to prevent them. In another enquiry—undertaken some years ago in the maternity ward of a big London hospital—much the same results were given. Mothers were asked, just before they left hospital and when they had had time to get fond of their babies, whether they had wanted to have the baby. Over half of them answered "No!"

The question arises as to why there are so many conceptions unwanted at the time they occur. Is it because parents, in spite of wishing not to have children, "leave things to chance," or is it because the methods chosen to prevent a conception are not reliable? The following answers, given by Mass Observation to the question

"Did you plan your family, or did you leave it to chance?" may perhaps throw some light on the intentions of the parents questioned at any rate. Of those married over ten years, whereas 37 per cent were in favour of some kind of planning, 41 per cent were prepared to "leave it to chance." The corresponding numbers for those who had been married five to ten years were 45 per cent who had wished to plan, and 32 per cent only who left it to chance. Of the newly married, 60 per cent were anxious to plan, and only 28 per cent to leave it to chance. Differences were also found between those with a secondary-school education and those with an elementary-school education. Of those with a secondary education, 63 per cent said families should be planned and 16 per cent said "leave it to chance." Of those with an elementary education, 42 per cent said families should be planned and 40 per cent were prepared to leave it to chance. It would appear, then, that it is the older women and those who have been less well educated who are least anxious to plan their families. This may be a reflection of the relative lack of knowledge of reliable methods of birth-control among these than among the younger and better educated.

The better-off mothers who can consult a doctor, or the comparatively few working-class mothers who attend birth-control clinics, know of methods at once reliable in their effects and harmless in use. But the methods usually adopted among the population at large, though sufficiently reliable to have been the means of bringing about the great fall in the birth-rate, are still insufficiently reliable to enable the wishes of a large number of parents to be carried out.

The many ways in which conceptions or births can be prevented have in most periods and in most countries always been known. They include abstention from intercourse, the use of the safe period, withdrawal, the use of contraceptives, and self-induced abortion.

(1) ABSTENTION FROM INTERCOURSE

Although "moral restraint" and late marriage was put forward by Malthus, writing in 1798, as one of the means by which a population should be kept down, it is regarded today as neither a practicable nor a desirable solution. Most people now hold the view that a normal sex life is good; and to deny it in married life except for purposes of procreation would run counter to today's standards of reasonable and right conduct. It should, however, be remembered that one of the reasons for today's smaller birth-rate may well be a change in marital habits. In the earlier periods there were few pleasures for the bulk of the population other than sex and drink. But since the development of wider interests, it is probable that, on the average, sexual intercourse takes place less frequently than before, and there is thus a reduced "exposure to risk" of pregnancy. The differential birth-rate between social classes may also partly be accounted for by differences in this respect.

(2) THE SAFE PERIOD

The practice of restricting intercourse to that part of the menstrual cycle when a woman is physiologically unable to conceive has probably had some effect on the birth-rate of Roman Catholics, amongst whom this method of family limitation is permissible. But since the characteristics of each woman in this respect are apt to differ and are not easy to find out, this method is not necessarily effective for any particular individual.

(3) CONCEPTION CONTROL

The most important means by which the fall in the birth-rate since 1875 has been brought about has undoubtedly been by the increase in the deliberate prevention of conceptions. The most widespread of the methods used is still that of withdrawal or "being careful," which, it is estimated, is practised by the majority of all those who aim at controlling conceptions at all. The part played by mechanical or chemical appliances is, contrary to the popular impression, relatively small—with the exception of the sheath, which I am told is being used to an increasing extent. The big change which started in 1875, therefore, was not so much the discovery of new methods as the spread of knowledge concerning old ones when such knowledge began to be considered no longer guilty or unmentionable. It is still extremely difficult to estimate the proportion of married couples in any class who use some form of conception- or birth-control.

The practice of birth-control undoubtedly started among the better-off sections of the community, with the result that for many decades their birth-rate was lower than that of the poorer sections. Now that the practice of birth-control has spread to all social classes except among the lowest group of subnormal families, the difference is very much less. We are here largely in the realm of surmises, but the number of unwanted conceptions already referred to would lead one to believe that, even apart from the social problem group, there are many women (especially among the poorer working classes) who are still ignorant of contraceptive methods, particularly of those which depend on the woman rather than on the man. It is to be hoped that, as a result of the enquiry now being carried out by the Royal Commission on Population on the use of contraceptive methods, considerable light will be thrown on this problem, and information on reliable contraceptive methods made available to those who need it most.

It should, of course, be remembered that because a baby is not wanted at any particular time, it does not follow that it may not be wanted later. An unwanted conception may only mean that the interval since the last child is shorter than the parents desired—not that they did not intend to have another child in the end.

But, as I pointed out before, the fact that there are still so many unwanted conceptions is highly significant. It must indicate that if the better forms of known contraceptives are substituted for less reliable ones, or if some form of contraceptive were to be discovered which would really be both foolproof and reliable, and if the wishes of the parents remained as they are today, this would—by preventing unwanted pregnancies—result in a fall of the birth-rate far greater than is usually anticipated.

(4) ILLEGAL ABORTION

The widespread practice of abortion, i.e. deliberate miscarriage, is generally admitted. It was estimated by the Inter-Departmental Committee on Abortion in 1939 that at least 16–20 per cent of pregnancies every year end in miscarriages. Of these it is thought that 40 per cent are deliberately terminated either through chemical or instrumental means used by the mothers themselves, or, in a smaller number of cases, by illegal operations of various kinds. According to the British Medical Association about 60,000 births a year are thus illegally prevented from occurring.

The risk to the mental and physical health of the mothers who undergo this ordeal, and to the fœtus when it is unsuccessful, is great. The fact that, in spite of this, such injurious methods are still employed serves to show both the strength of the parents' desire not to have the child concerned, and the lack of use or failure of contraceptive methods. It is not easy to ascertain whether the numbers of abortions have increased or fallen since 1875, but the remedies for this unhappy state of affairs can only be both an increased desire for children and the spread of knowledge of safe and harmless methods of contraception.

Part III

THE CONSEQUENCES OF A DECLINING POPULATION

Chapter 11

PERSONAL, SOCIAL AND POLITICAL CONSEQUENCES

"Let not England forget her precedence of teaching nations how to live."—(*Milton*.)

"The stability of England is the security of the modern world—the English stand for liberty."—(*Emerson*.)

I HAVE shown that there are at present many indications that population trends, once the immediate effect of the war and of demobilisation have passed, will revert to what they were in 1939. The most likely prospect before us is, then, that a gradual decline will set in a few years hence, and that, since the children who will be the parents of the next generation are already born, and we know that they are fewer in number than their own parents, we can be virtually certain that thirty years hence there will be a smaller population than today. Thereafter, unless 1939 tendencies are reversed, this will only be the beginning of a continuing decline. If gloomier prophecies with regard to a lower birth-rate and a higher death-rate materialise—and this seems to me very probable—the decline in the population will be on a larger scale than any estimate that has so far been made. Though we cannot predict an exact time-scale, as long as the average family is two or less, the population must ultimately fade out unless falling numbers are made good by immigration.

It is therefore of the utmost importance to try to answer the questions "Does this matter? and if so, why?" This involves estimating, as far as we can, the consequences—personal and social, political and economic—of our population's declining at various rates and over different periods of time. But the question *must* be answered, since the more perturbed we are at the future prospects, the sooner should we take steps aimed at arresting the anticipated trends. If, on the other hand, we seriously consider that there is nothing alarming about the situation, we cannot be blamed if we continue to ignore it.

We have, therefore, to try to estimate what is likely to happen, first thirty years hence, when we are virtually certain that if the 1939 trends return the population of England and Wales will be somewhere about 38 millions; and next—if the same trends continue—for further generations to come. Our questions, therefore, must be answered. For although it is too late, whatever we do, to affect the numbers of the next generation, the adoption *now* of well-conceived and wise policies on the part of the Government may, if backed by a changed public opinion, help to arrest the decline about that point.

There are many who remember long queues outside the Employment Exchange in pre-war years, and fear to see them beginning again later. There are many also who note the bad results of congested ways of living in our bigger towns, the waste and worry of traffic jams and the sprawl over the countryside, and think that our land, with a density of 703 people to the square mile, is physically too small for its population. All these will hail the idea of a smaller population with a cheer. It is indeed conceivable that today we may be already over-populated; and certainly the four or five million less we are likely to be in another thirty years will bring certain definite advantages to the nation, and make it easier, for instance, to solve the problems of food supply, of housing, transport, exports and imports during that period. So this prospect in itself is by no means alarming.

But once started the decline is likely to continue further, and this would be quite another matter, as I shall try to show later.

It is, in any case, far more likely that some at least of the very real contemporary troubles complained of—such as over-congestion and a feared return of unemployment—are due, not to the numbers of our people, but to bad organisation or sheer lack of organisation; and that we could have in this country a population as large as or even considerably larger than at present, and yet free ourselves from these particular difficulties.

THE PERSONAL ISSUE

Before embarking further on national issues, let us consider the effects of a declining population on the individual family, the average size of which would be even smaller than today. Small families—other things being equal—can offer as a rule a far less rich and interesting family life than can larger ones—even though their standard of living per head may be higher. Where there are only one or two children, these often suffer from over-anxiety on the part of their parents or from a lack of salutary companionship themselves. The practical and psychological difficulties involved in bringing up an only child, or a child separated by several years from a brother and sister, are now being appreciated by an increasing number of parents. The two wars, with their heavy toll of only sons or only children, have emphasised the danger of parents' putting all their eggs in one basket. Generally speaking, families with several children are likely to have more healthy emotional satisfactions, a more robust view of life and a more entertaining family circle than is the case in a small family.

It is a truism that the pleasures usually labelled "a good time" tend to evaporate as time passes. But the rearing of children being a creative process, remains, as do all creative processes, of absorbing and changing interest throughout life. Each child brings his own individual qualities, capacities and interests to the general pool, and it is common knowledge that children of large families—except in cases where there has been grinding poverty—nearly always testify to the fun they have had in their own homes. School-teachers, moreover, often observe that members of a large family are frequently better mixers, more co-operative and more independent than is the only darling.

At the other end of life, old people usually find their main interest in the members of their family—though the former need to have children to support a parent in old age is passing, as retirement and old-age pensions grow more adequate.

THE PHILOSOPHIC ASPECT

Is Life Worth Living?

This is a fundamental issue, and we must approach it first from the philosophic angle and ask what would be likely to happen if the shrinkage in our population continued with cumulatively greater effects for a series of generations, leading inevitably to ultimate extinction, or to absorption in very different kinds of peoples. Is this something we can face with equanimity?

We must then ask the further question, "Does it matter if human life stops?" This is by no means an imaginary danger. As will be shown in a later chapter, the small-family pattern is not peculiar to this country. It is the rule already among the nations in North-west Europe, in most of our Dominions and in the U.S.A. In all these countries, as well as in this one, if no relevant changes occur, a fading out of the population may be expected sooner or later. It is also anticipated that nations such as the U.S.S.R. and other countries in Eastern Europe, Egypt and Japan—whose populations are now increasing by leaps and bounds on account of an unrestricted birth-rate, combined with a declining death-rate—will later on follow the same route if and when they reach a stage in their social and industrial development like our present one. This is likely to be eventually the case even in such countries as India and China* which are still in the earlier states of development in which birth- and death-rates are both high. Should, indeed, our own pre-war situation as regards population at long last become universalised—and judging by the spread of the small-family pattern in Europe this is at least possible—the human race must eventually follow the dodo into oblivion.

Whether this does or does not matter is not something which can be argued about. It is a matter of fundamental faith and of one's psychological outlook. If life on the whole seems to be good and purposeful— even if at times for all and all the time for some it involves hideous suffering and frustration—if one can sometimes at least echo Browning's words:

"How good is man's life, the mere living! How fit
to employ
All the heart and the soul and the senses, for ever
in joy!"

* See Chapter 22.

then the prospect of the fading out of the human race or of any worthy representatives of it would be both the ultimate tragedy and present challenge.

The Place of the British Nation

A further question, the answer to which is fundamentally a matter of faith, relates specifically to our own country. Is there any special reason why—whatever happens to the rest of the world—the British nation as it is now constituted should survive? If this threatened decline materialises, so that in a few centuries our numbers have shrunk to a population a third of its present size, it is hardly likely that this green and pleasant land would be left unoccupied, even if it should carry a far smaller population than today. Pressure from the Near and Far East—where it may take generations before the planned small family becomes the accepted pattern—may well mean that an emptying Britain would be largely occupied by people from nations with very different traditions and ideas from our own.

Now it will be generally agreed that every great nation has its own unique contribution to make to the world's stock of qualities and ideals. The British people have traditions and standards of value—ethical, religious and political—derived from a conviction of the value of each individual as a person. These democratic ideals of freedom, of kindness, of justice, of reason and of the rule of law are needed more than ever in a world in which many countries have not as yet discovered how to combine freedom with order. Should the Mother Country, therefore, fade out of existence or become too greatly outnumbered by peoples with different characteristics, or should Britons become so few in number that we no longer had the influence and prestige of a great Power, our country could no longer be in the position that she is in today—as the centre of a great Commonwealth—to spread the ideals in which we believe, and the world would inevitably be very much the poorer. Victor Gollancz, in *Our Threatened Values,* puts this strongly as follows:

"Love of country is a curious thing; as in other sorts of love, it attributes qualities to the beloved which may not in fact be there. But I cannot escape the conviction, when all has been said, that there are in this country reserves of moral leadership that can still save the world, if only we can rise to the full height of the argument. . . .

". . . My friends from the Continent, and not from Germany or other defeated countries alone, have often told me that when they land on an English shore or at an English airport, they feel they have come to Paradise. They are not referring to our food, or our law and order, or our relative prosperity: they are thinking of our freedom, of our—may I say it?—decency, of, in Mr. Churchill's words: 'Our customs and our nature.' . . . I do believe that they are right. I do believe that, corrupted though we may be by war and its aftermath, there is still something in the air we breathe, still some moral source deep in our cities and our countryside, which no other people in the modern world has the good fortune to possess."

General Smuts' broadcast in Victory Week 1946 summed up admirably the place the British Commonwealth could fill:

"Scattered, sprawling over the seas, the British group might yet prove the saving grace of this vast Power constellation—the area of stability between the two Power poles. Let neither Great Americans nor Great Russians look upon it as a danger, as something menacing their greatness. Rather is it a necessary feature of our whole world set-up. . . . Let them accept it and look upon it as an integral part of world security, no less than U.N.O. itself."

In this book I intend to make the assumptions both that life is on the whole good, and that the British nation with its mixture of races and the influence it exerts on world affairs is abundantly worth conserving. Those who disagree with these propositions will therefore waste their time if they read on.

THE PSYCHOLOGICAL ASPECT

Psychologically, it must indeed be a depressing experience to belong to a community which lacks the vitality and spirit to reproduce itself. It is not easy to imagine what to belong to a steadily decreasing and ageing population on a national scale would be like—quite a different experience from belonging to one which has never been large. We have never experienced it in this country since the days of the Black Death. But the depopulation of the Highlands or of Ireland during the last hundred years, and the continuing decline in the number of people in many parts of our countryside, have shown us on a smaller scale something of what "a Britain shrinking within its skin" would mean. A declining school population, due to the lower birth-rate of the thirties, which resulted in our entering this war with 2 million children fewer than at the beginning of the last, had indeed already become widespread before the war. Should this process be continued over two or three generations, in the course of time many buildings, factories, roads and railways would inevitably become unwanted and the cheerful bustle of many of our familiar ways of living would have disappeared. Social and cultural amenities, such as a sufficient variety of schools, churches, hospitals and cultural activities, which are inevitably based on comparatively large numbers of people living close to one another, can now only be supplied in districts with a fairly large aggregate population. With a population continuing to decline, such districts are bound to become fewer, and only holiday-makers who are dedicated to solitude would rejoice.

There is, of course, the other alternative. Instead of actually declining, our population may be, in fact, maintained by immigrants, who—since the North-west European countries will probably also have declining populations—will probably come from Eastern Europe, and perhaps also from Asia. We should then inevitably find ourselves involved in many difficult problems arising from efforts to assimilate a large number of people with different attitudes towards life from our own; and we should end up as a people with a very different ethnic make-up and national characteristics from those we have today. It is questionable whether this would constitute an improvement. These problems are dealt with at greater length in Chapter 21, on Migration.

POLITICAL CONSEQUENCES

(1) Britain's Position in the World

To return to this question, Britain has up to now been regarded as a first-class Power, with considerable influence on and responsibilities for the political and economic developments in the world as a whole. But even today there are signs of this being questioned. Will the anticipated decline in population reduce us to a second- or to a third-class Power either in the next generation or later? Will it be necessary in the future, as it has often been in the past, for a nation to attain a certain size in order that not only her standard of living, but her national status and influence may be assured?

Certainly, a country's status and her influence bear no very close relationship to the size of her population. Today, for instance, the position of this country in the world is "based more on her advantages and her strategic position, her highly developed political and economic institutions and her being the centre of the British Commonwealth than on her numbers." * A small decline in the population is not likely to affect any of these factors very much. But the steady decline we are envisaging is bound to affect them all. It must be remembered that Great Britain's 46 million must be compared with the 174 million of Russia (still increasing very quickly—they will probably be 300 million in the year 2000), the 140 million of the United States, the 400 million of India and a probably even larger population in China. It may be that a Britain with 30 million or fewer can no longer be counted among the great Powers. Size, however, is not the only consideration. China, with her comparative industrial backwardness, has not yet developed into a first-class military Power, though she may well do so in time to come. But since war is becoming more and more a question of the industrial power behind the front line, a country with a highly developed industry which can produce the munitions of war, and whose fighting forces are skilled and intelligent may well compensate to a great extent for lack of numbers. As Mr. Winston Churchill said: "The future of the world is to the highly educated races, who alone can handle the scientific apparatus necessary for pre-eminence in peace or sur-

* P.E.P. Planning.

vival in war. Above all, atomic energy punctuates the whole structure of military strategy with a gigantic question mark."

It may be, therefore, that what affects the prosperity and strength of a nation both in peace and in war is not, within certain limits, the total numbers so much as the numbers of those who, by virtue of their intelligence, their standards of value, their education, their general competence and strength of character, are the leaders of the people in the widest sense and fit to direct policy in every walk of national life. A country with a comparatively small population may have as many suited to be leaders in this sense as has a country with a much larger population, but which has lower standards and less wealth per head, fewer traditions and fewer opportunities for education. But there are limits to this process. The requisite numbers of such leaders would not in their turn be likely to be forthcoming unless the matrix constituted by the total population was at any rate of a certain size, and had also the virility to maintain its numbers before it became too small. If, indeed, its birth-rate were to fall below replacement level, the numbers of men young enough to be among the producing and fighting ages would shrink more than in proportion to the whole population. This position is already clearly visible in this country. We are finding it difficult to secure the 750,000 or so needed for the Forces and our industries are crying out for more workers. It has been reckoned that by the year 2000 the age-group of men between 15 and 35 would, if our pre-war trends continued, number just half what it did in 1939. We would then be bound to become a second- or third-class Power.

The theory that a nation which fails to reproduce itself and is increasing in its average age is decadent, and will be replaced by younger and more vigorous nations, was already before the war a real factor in international affairs. Germany must have realised in 1939 that her striking power was at its peak in relation to the rest of Europe. Her population was already twice that of France, but she was frightened both of Poland and the U.S.S.R., who were showing a startling increase in the numbers of population of fighting age, whilst Germany —like ourselves—was heading for a smaller population, especially as regards men in the fighting age-groups. We ourselves should indeed have been in a parlous position during the last war if we had not had the support, not only of the Commonwealth, but also of Allies with far bigger populations than our own.

It may indeed be that the ideals towards which U.N.O. is striving—that the rights and institutions of both small and large Powers can be safeguarded—will be carried out in practice. But there is a growing realisation that only through the possession of force on the part of peace-loving nations will U.N.O. succeed in preventing war. The League of Nations failed through lack of an understanding of this fact. However far aggression, militarism or imperialism may be from the minds of our people, no one in this Year of Grace can dare guarantee a peaceful future. A continuously declining population in this country, with an accentuated decline in the younger age-groups, cannot then help being an alarming proposition.

(2) *Britain as the Centre of the Commonwealth*

It was a Britain growing more rapidly than other European Powers which built the Empire and became for more than a century the determining factor in world policy. Her growing numbers also enabled the Dominions to be peopled almost entirely from the

Mother Country (with the exception of the early French settlers in Canada and the Boers in South Africa). As things have turned out, most of the Dominions—in particular Australia and New Zealand—have population trends much like our own (see Chapter 23). In relation to their resources they are still under-populated and are looking to this country to continue to supply them with young people. We, however, shall not have the people—especially the young people—to spare to mitigate their under-population, unless we deliberately adopt the policy of looking at the British Commonwealth so much as one unit that we are content to let numbers fall here and to build up new centres in Canada or Australia. If their present under-population continues, the result may well be that the anticipated pressure of people from the over-populated countries of Asia may, with or without war, eventually overflow into Canada, Australia and New Zealand, which have so far only been able to keep them out by immigration laws which in later years it might not be easy to maintain. The teeming peoples of India in particular would in any case have a strong moral claim for entry.

With regard to the non-self-governing parts of the Empire, and to those just promoted to self-government, there is still a great demand for young men and, more lately, for young women from this country to help with their development—whether as administrators, teachers, doctors, nurses, social workers or skilled artisans. These are the inescapable responsibilities accepted by our people in earlier decades and which we cannot refuse to honour, even if it means depleting our own resources.

(3) *Age-grouping of the Electorate*

We can assume that considerable changes in our political and social life will arise from a declining population. But it is not too easy to see what these might be. Perhaps the most important will be due to changes in the age distribution of the electorate, which it is estimated will be as follows:

Table 12.— Percentage Approximate Age Composition of the Electorate of England and Wales, 1939–99

	20–29 YEARS	30–59 YEARS	60 YEARS AND OVER
1939	22·1	59·9	18·0
1959	18·0	59·5	22·5
1979	15·7	54·8	29·5
1999	12·2	52·9	34·9

On the basis of this estimate in 1999 the over fifties would comprise 53 per cent of the total voting population. This may both bring about a shift in the relative strength of various political groups and may affect the policy within each of these groups. Young voters are said to prefer the more "progressive" political parties, whereas age is considered more conservative. If this is true, the parties which are considered progressive are likely to lose votes, while those which prefer gradual evolution of existing institutions to radical changes may gain in power.

There will also inevitably be a change in emphasis from interest in the welfare of young people and children to interest in that of older people. Political pressure will be increasingly exercised by those largely preoccupied with the problems of old age. The long delay in providing family allowances, and their small amount in contradistinction to the retirement pensions, shows that this tendency is already present.

It is, of course, important to keep a balanced policy between young and old. Unless adequate provision is made for the young, in due course the productive power of the nation will suffer and be unable to make adequate provision for the old. But unless the older members of the community feel that they are being treated fairly—or even generously—it may well be that they would oppose a policy of spending more on the young. The real solution of the apparent conflict between an active-population policy and the interests of the elderly is to be found in adapting conditions of employment so that older people can be kept in work and off pensions for as long as possible.

ADVANTAGES OF A SMALL POPULATION

It may be that in setting out so many of the disadvantages of a declining population, I may be accused of not having taken into account the many advantages of living in a country with a small population, such as Holland, Belgium, the Scandinavian countries or New Zealand—and advantages there undoubtedly are. Problems of government are simpler, since it is easier to find men who can tackle the problems of a small people adequately than men who can deal with those of a large nation. It is in New Zealand, with its population of $1\frac{1}{2}$ millions in a country as big as Great Britain, that the standard of living is higher than anywhere else in the world; it is in Sweden and Switzerland that democracy appears to be most creative; in Sweden, again, that art enters most into everyday life. It is Holland with its heritage of magnificent art and architecture which has much to teach us today as regards administration, in particular in public health. And it must not be forgotten that it was two small nations, the Jews and the Greeks, who gave to the world its greatest religious and its greatest intellectual heritages.

It is not surprising, therefore, that there are many who ask, "What care I for the big battalions? Is not life in a second- or third-class Power—which cannot aspire to be influential in world affairs and can devote all its attention to setting its own house in order—a much more peaceful and satisfactory kind of existence than that in a big Power actively taking part in the international ferment?" This may have been true before the war, but it is hardly true any longer. The war showed the small countries to be entirely at the mercy of the bigger ones. Holland, Belgium, Norway and Denmark were overrun; Switzerland and Sweden only escaped because it suited Hitler to keep them more as sources of supply than as conquered territories. Their freedom today is due only to their having bigger Powers behind them to fight their battles on their behalf, and "realism" in politics is not likely to give them much of a look in as regards their own destinies. There will be a long, long road for U.N.O. to travel before this is changed.

Chapter 12

ECONOMIC CONSEQUENCES

IT is no easy matter to separate the effect of changes in the size of a population from those of other changes in its economic life, since—whether a population is increasing or declining or remaining the same—both its actual numbers and the extent and rate at which they may be changing are only two or three among the vast complex of factors which together determine the level of national prosperity. Moreover, the mere complexity of these factors makes it extremely difficult to foretell the result of changes in any of them taken singly; any connection there is between numbers and existing prosperity is indirect, and takes place as a result of a complex of economic and social relationships as a whole.

This has not always been so. Among more primitive communities largely dependent on agriculture, where technical inventions are few and far between and capital equipment plays a comparatively unimportant part, this connection is much closer. It is a commonplace of economic science that although at first more labour on a piece of land increases the produce, after a certain point the produce from any given area increases less in proportion to additional amounts of labour and capital applied—even though this may facilitate greater specialisation and therefore more expert work.

It was this kind of community with which Malthus was familiar when, in 1798, he put forward the view that in the end population always tends to increase more quickly than the resources of any particular country, and that checks to unlimited population increase are inevitably brought about by the lack of food and other material sources as well as by war or disease. With regard to this country, his contentions proved to be not so much wrong as out of date. In the event his gloomy prophecies never materialised, as shortly after he wrote we began to be able to draw sources of food supply and raw materials from the Americas and Australasia. We were also able to reap the advantages of greatly increased technical inventions and improvements. Indeed, in the period of our most rapid population expansion during the nineteenth century, our standards of living continually rose. Although the number of consumers between 1833 and 1893 was rising by something between 1 and $1\frac{1}{2}$ per cent per year, the growth in real income (that is in the amount of goods and services per head) during the same period rose by a great deal more.

In examining the probable effects of a declining population on our economic situation, we must here again distinguish between the small fall we anticipate in a generation's time and the effects of the much greater fall which must be anticipated later if, in the meantime, the 1939 population trends are not reversed. We must also bear in mind the different effects of a population which is continuing to shrink and one which becomes stabilised—though at a lower level than today.

Bearing this in mind, therefore, let us try to estimate what in the future is likely to be the connection between smaller numbers and (1) unemployment, (2) national resources, (3) age distribution, (4) cost of social services, (5) burdens on public expenditure, and (6) the export trade.

(1) UNEMPLOYMENT

Although the acute problem today is how to obtain more man-power, the fear is always present that when immediate post-war industrial conditions are ended, unemployment on a considerable scale may return for a variety of reasons, and may increase in amount as concentration on essential industries is worked.

The man in the street not unnaturally regards unemployment as due to there being too many people; the more widespread it is, the more does he welcome a smaller population. He does not realise that general unemployment bears little relation to the actual numbers of the people. Smaller numbers may mean fewer competitors for work, but they also mean a smaller home market, which is bound to lead to a lower demand for certain goods, even though a rising standard of life may provide a market for others. It must not be forgotten that every producer is at the same time a consumer, and that each baby who comes into the world has a mouth to be filled and other needs to be met both before and after it becomes ready for work.

Let us, however, examine some different types of unemployment to see what relation each may bear to a population decline.

Frictional or Temporary Unemployment

This in no way depends on the size of the population, since it is impossible in an imperfect world for the right job always to be found in the right place at the right time. "There is no vacancy," as an Employment Exchange official said to an old student of mine who had only recently emerged from a mental home and said she wanted a job as Prime Minister! Casual and seasonal types of work also lead to this kind of unemployment and need to be dealt with by better organisation of the trades concerned.

Structural Unemployment

Population changes are of greater importance when considering unemployment in individual industries caused by changes in their technique or in the demand for their products. Between the two wars unemployment in the coal, cotton and shipbuilding industries, concentrated largely in the "special" areas, was mainly of this type. A declining birth-rate involves, of course, a decline in the number of children as compared with older people; but the main expenditure of a family is for the urgent needs of children—food, clothing and house-room—demands for which are stable and call for few changes in the industries concerned. Where the average number of children in a family is fewer, parents are more likely to spend a larger proportion of their income on luxury goods or services with respect to which changes in demand are more frequent, and unemployment apt to arise from fashion's whims.

In a population with many young people, changes in demand for labour in individual industries take the form, not so much of discharging older men as of the young entrants to industry making for trades which are expanding, rather than for those which are declining. It is, moreover, much easier for the younger workers already in a shrinking industry to move where work is more plentiful; since they, unlike the older workers, are not yet encumbered by family or home. Where, however, the birth-rate is declining and there is therefore a reduction in the proportion of young people, changes in the nature of employment will be more at the cost of older workers whose mobility is limited.

Mass Unemployment

The high rate of general unemployment, such as accompanied the depression in the early thirties, was, however, only in part due to unemployment in particular industries, important though this was. It is now considered that the main cause for unemployment in nearly all industries at the same time is a lack of the right relationship between investment and spending. If there is no outlet in the shape of investment for the savings people have made, or if they are frightened that these will not bring in adequate returns when invested, the investment does not take place. Capital goods are not produced, and unemployment ensues in the first place both in industries which make machinery, tractors, etc., and those which use them. Keynes reckoned that nearly half the additions to our stock of capital in the nineteenth century was in response to the needs of new consumers arising from an increased population in this country, together with a corresponding rise in the population in other countries which bought our goods. It was this demand continuously rising—partly on account of larger numbers of people and partly of a higher standard of living— which in the past contributed greatly towards promoting periods in which trade was good, and towards helping this country to emerge comparatively quickly from periods of depression.

What is likely to happen in the future with a probably declining population and a possibly reduced demand for our exports from the rest of the world? It is by no means easy to say—especially as it must always be borne in mind that a change in numbers is only one among so many unknowns both in this country and abroad. If the decline in numbers results in a declining market all round, investors will be less ready on that account to take risks, since demands for goods and services will tend to be below what could be produced. Employers will not feel enough confidence with regard to the making of profits, and a pessimistic atmosphere may be the result. On the other hand, better industrial organisation, more enterprising business methods, more efficient technique and lower rates of interest may well more than make up for lower numbers and provide new outlets for investments which would be sufficient to absorb all our savings, and thus reduce the likelihood of unemployment. Whether this happier prospect will materialise or not depends partly on the level of savings, out of which investments are made, but still more on the measures taken by the Government to promote the accepted policy of maintaining a high level of employment. This can probably be achieved both by the Government's demanding more goods and services itself, and by its taking steps to stimulate a demand among both producers and consumers by such measures as a reduction in the rate of interest, and a redistribution of incomes through subsidies or social insurance.

If, however, any population decline continues beyond the next generation, so that this country finds itself with a considerably smaller population than that of to-day, though the prevention of unemployment would remain still a question of organisation rather than of numbers, it would become a much more difficult task to carry out.

(2) NATIONAL RESOURCES

In an agricultural country it is true that, once a certain point has been reached, the larger the number of workers on the land, the less per head is likely to be the return for their labour. In the same way, after a certain amount of capital has been spent, the less is the return on subsequent investments. In the countries of Eastern Europe, for instance, the low standard of living before the war was largely due to there being too many people in relation to the amount of agricultural land and the methods of agriculture. But in industrialised countries like our own, where so long as peace prevailed we did not even try to grow enough food for more than half our population, this law of diminishing returns, as it is called, does not hold. Up to now the average income per head of the population has more than kept pace with the growth of the amount of capital invested—a sure sign that we are not over-populated. Our highly developed industrial system is increasingly based on mass production, which allows for the manufacture of sufficient goods to exchange for the raw material and the food imported from abroad.

A continuous series of technical inventions has resulted in a greatly increased productivity per head in this country, and each year sees more and more labour-saving devices, though, compared with America, there is still considerable room for the introduction of new mechanised processes in our factories, farms and mines. Assuming this happens, a reduction in our labour force is not likely for some years to come in itself to bring about a lower standard of living, as it may well be compensated for by greater industrial efficiency.

But the urgent need for more production leads to a concern about the numbers of our men and women of working age. We cannot even now muster the number of workers we need both for our exports and our home industries, together with the defence force of 750,000 our military experts consider the very minimum necessary. There is already a marked lack of certain kinds of labour, such as in the mines, on the land, and in nursing and domestic service, to satisfy which we are allowing workers to come in from abroad. With a continuously declining population the number of industries which can only be adequately manned through immigration will increase. France has been in this position for some time. Immigration on the scale which might become necessary is, however, in our own case likely to be actively resented by public opinion. I will return to this question in Chapter 22.

If we look farther ahead the prospect is definitely gloomy. If the numbers of our working population begin to fall, with no compensating immigration, there will surely come a time, even if delayed for several generations, when there will not be enough workers to allow for the use of modern methods of mass production to anything like the same extent as today—and later possibly not at all. Australia finds its population of 7 millions far too small to develop as many industries on mass-production lines as she would like, and the same situation would undoubtedly arise here if we had very many fewer workers than we have today.

(3) ECONOMIC EFFECTS OF CHANGES IN AGE DISTRIBUTION

The effects of a declining birth-rate on the age distribution of the population have been described, and it suffices here to point out that "at the beginning of the century one Briton in three was a child under 15 and less than one in fifteen had reached pensionable age. It is quite probable that if 1939 trends continue, in twenty-five years' time only one in six will be a child, whereas one in five will have reached retirement age. At the same period workers between 45 and 64 will have outnumbered those under 30 by three to two." *

The Government Actuary tells us that in 1944 there were over $5\frac{1}{2}$ million men and women of pensionable

* R. Titmuss.

age, and that these are likely to increase by nearly 2 millions by 1984. After this time their numbers, though not their proportion, would start once more to decline, owing to the smaller birth-rate from 1924 onwards. The effect of these large numbers of old people on the cost of National Insurance will be formidable unless the retirement age is considerably raised. Not only does it mean that by 1975 there will be thirty-one pensioners to every hundred contributors, whereas today there are only sixteen; but by 1978 retirement pensions will be costing £501 millions out of the £749 millions which is the total estimated expenditure on all benefits, including administration. In other words, two-thirds of the total estimated cost of all insurance benefits will be for retirement pensions.

This large and increasing proportion of elderly people may also have other drawbacks. It is, for instance, usually considered that middle-aged and elderly people have not the flexibility and adaptability of the young. And yet both these qualities will be more than ever required if this country is to face successfully the many and complex problems of reconstruction and of the development of our industry. On the other hand, it is generally held that wisdom comes with the years. Bernard Shaw observed, round about his ninetieth birthday, that he would not consider himself wise enough to have any responsible part in governing the country until he had attained the age of 150. Ripe experience is certainly as essential as youthful enterprise. Moreover, the growing mechanisation of industry and agriculture will bring in methods of production more suitable for older people.

Fortunately, also, the higher expectation of life today ensures that a larger proportion of the elderly than in previous times are hale and hearty enough to go on with productive work long after the minimum age for retirement pensions has been reached.

At the present moment, owing to the low birth-rate of the thirties, there are relatively few dependent children; while the proportion of old people, though higher than in the past, is lower than it will be in future years. Thus the number of dependents—children and old people together—per hundred adults has gradually fallen from seventy in 1881 (mostly children) to forty-nine in 1939 (mostly old people). But the proportion of elderly dependents will gradually increase as the proportion of old people increases. The cost of maintaining a child is much less than that of keeping an old person; so that it involves a greater burden on the country's workers to support dependents when these include a large proportion of old people than when the majority are young children. If, in the end, as we hope, the present birth-rate trends are reversed as a result of the adoption of population policies to be suggested later, and the proportion of children again increases, this would lead to an even heavier burden of dependents, consisting as it would both of many children and many old people at the same time. From the point of view of the community it is indeed far more encouraging to spend money on children, since this expenditure can be regarded as a hopeful investment, than to spend it on old people—desirable as this may be from the point of view of individual happiness.

(4) EFFECT OF A DECLINING POPULATION ON THE COST OF THE SOCIAL SERVICES

(i) Education

It might be expected that a diminished expenditure on education, due to an ever smaller number of children, would help to compensate for the higher expenditure on pensions and old-age homes; but no proportionate decrease of this kind is likely to take place. To be efficient, schools must keep a certain number of grades, so that smaller numbers of children should mean emptier rather than fewer classrooms. Different types of schools and of other educational institutions must be provided within reasonable distance of the homes of the children who attend them, even though the number of children is fewer, and the increased use of motor transport may allow schools to be situated at a greater distance than at present from some of the homes.

For many years to come, then, the need for a reduction in the size of the classes, together with the longer school life provided both for the under fives and the over fourteens by the 1944 Education Act, means that there can be no economy in the number of teachers. But if the number of children continues to fall, the situation will change. Many school buildings will undoubtedly be scrapped, and it will be far more difficult to persuade the more parsimonious local education authorities to put up new buildings of better design and material—if there are many old ones unused, and if even the new ones may later on not be required. Comparatively few new young teachers will be appointed; numbers will be so much reduced that children of many age-groups will have to be taught together, which usually results in less efficiency. At a school I know in Cornwall where two generations ago there used to be 250 children, there are now only fifty. These are lumped together in only two classes, taken by the head and his assistant, and proper grading is impossible.

(ii) Housing

Much the same situation will occur with regard to housing. We may well feel that any slackening in the present practically unlimited demand for houses will be a relief. For in spite of the slowing down of the growth of the population today and the small average size of the family, the total number of individual families is still getting larger, owing to the great increase in the number of marriages in the last few years. (It should be noted that "family" in the census sense of the word means a separate household of one or more people.) The total number of families in this country is now about 12 millions, having increased by about 2 millions since 1930; and although the peak in this respect has probably been reached, it is not expected that these numbers will go down by any appreciable amount for many years to come.

As we have already pointed out, there is a special need for houses large enough for the bigger families we hope to see. There is also a need for many small houses for elderly people living singly or in couples. But, as in the case of the schools, what is likely to happen is that there will be fewer people per house rather than fewer houses. Again, as in the case of schools, there is an urgent need to replace substandard buildings, and it may be at least a generation before these needs can be satisfied.

But if we look beyond this period to a population declining still further, although replacement both of houses and equipment will continue to be necessary as standards rise, we shall probably find ourselves with far too many houses on our hands. A considerable part of the building industry will have to be employed in demolition if the town and countryside are not to be strewn with derelict and unwanted buildings; in any case, a more drastic shrinkage in the numbers in the building industry will result than would be the case if the population remained stationary.

(5) BURDENS ON PUBLIC EXPENDITURE

If, as I have suggested, the cost of the social services (and I should also add the provision of adequate defence services) is by no means likely to decline to the extent to which the population declines, the State will find it increasingly difficult to raise the revenue required for its many commitments. The smaller number of workers of productive age may well be reflected in reduced production, which would lessen the buoyancy of the national revenue to which we have been accustomed as long as production is on the increase. It is unlikely, moreover, that the National Debt will have decreased anything like as much as the population is likely to do during the next twenty or thirty years. It will therefore constitute a heavier burden per head at that time, even if the interest should fall in the meantime.

(6) BRITAIN AND INTERNATIONAL TRADE

Great Britain has now for nearly a hundred years supported a far higher population by means of world trade than could be maintained if she had had to depend on her own resources alone, and since the war the question is often put whether our position might not be strengthened by a smaller population. It is pointed out that the 40 per cent increase over pre-war exports the present situation requires could be reduced if there were a smaller population, since so large a proportion of the imports exchanged against these exports is on account of foodstuffs and raw materials. Every additional mouth over the number that can be fed from home-grown resources increases the need for additional exports by that amount. It is further pointed out that the demand for British manufactures is likely to be reduced in the future—in the first place, because Britain "has spent and overspent her reserves of international purchasing power as the price of winning two wars"; and secondly, because so many countries, formerly mainly agricultural with only foodstuffs to export, are becoming industrialised, thus making fewer demands on our industry and having less food to export. What can be urged on the other side?

"To say that Britain should accept a reduction of population in order to avoid pressure on her balance of payments which may continue after the present emergency is in a sense an admission that Britain, despite her level of education, despite her technical skill which could produce Mulberry Harbours, Radar, penicillin, despite her administrative skill, is unable to adjust her economy to the conditions to be expected in the second half of the twentieth century. There are no technical reasons for such a conclusion. . . . It is in the quality, the skill and education of the British people that our main asset lies, and if this quality is properly and fully developed, it should prove an asset quite comparable to the start which Britain attained in the cruder forms of mechanisation a hundred years ago. It is true that a reduction of say 10 millions in population would reduce Britain's need of imports and her gross reliance on international trade. But it is probable that an increase of population would more than feed itself and leave a margin to be devoted to raising the general standard of life. . . . An expansion in world economy is surely due, and Britain, with her high technical ability and administrative skill, should be able to seize this opportunity. It is a question of national willpower and national initiative, not a question of immutable economic laws." (*"Planning," No. 251, issued by P.E.P.*)

SUMMARY OF PART III

To sum up, therefore, I have shown that, in trying to estimate the results of a declining and ageing population, it is necessary to differentiate between the effects in the next generation (say thirty years hence, in which the anticipated reduction will probably be in the order of 4 or 5 millions) and those in the more distant future in which—provided the net reproduction rate again falls to below one—the population will become ever smaller and older. This will be inevitable except on the unlikely possibility that immigration takes place on a very big scale.

The effect on the individual of an even smaller average family than now would, it was suggested, lead to a far less rich and happy family life than might otherwise be the case—all the more as the refusal to have more than one or two children would often indicate a lack of belief in the future of self and country, and a lack of faith in life itself.

It was also emphasised that a Britain with a much smaller population would no longer be an important influence in world affairs, either in peace or war; she would lose her status and power, with all that implies as regards the welfare of the Commonwealth and of the world.

With regard to economic consequences, it was shown that a declining population is not likely to offer any relief with regard to unemployment, since this does not bear any direct relation to actual numbers of workers, but depends rather on industrial organisation. Smaller home markets and an older and less enterprising population is, if anything, likely to have a depressing effect, other things being equal, on employment prospects. It is impossible to say what the effect of a small population is likely to be on standards of living, since these depend on so many factors other than the size of the population. In the immediate future a smaller demand for imports of food would offer some relief; but if the decline continues and the population of this country becomes very much smaller, the whole character of our industrial organisation would have to be changed.

Part IV

POLICIES

Chapter 13

THE TARGET

WHAT size population do we want? Curiously enough, this is a question it is impossible to answer. It is easy to say what we *don't* want, since this would include both a rapidly increasing population and one which, however slowly it might start on a downward slope, would inevitably decline more or less rapidly as time passes—like going down a waterchute. And yet it looks as if the latter is the course for which we are set, unless a drastic change in the average family size sets in.

THE IDEAL OR OPTIMUM POPULATION

We cannot definitely state the ideal number of people for this country. In any highly industrialised country there are so many factors concerned that we cannot tell at any given moment what the ideal should be. In theory, indeed, there is such an ideal or "optimum," as it is called. Or rather there are several ideals at the same time, according as to whether we are considering, for instance, the economic aspect (the amount of wealth per head); or the social aspect (the number that will allow for the pleasantest conditions of daily life); or the strategic aspect (the number sufficient to enable us to keep the armed forces which any given political situation might necessitate).

In practice, however, we cannot know whether or when we have reached any of these ideals. Take, for instance, the economic optimum. What this means in theory is the number of people in a given country, at a given time, with a given amount of capital and practical skill, who would be able to live at a standard higher than if their number were either more or less. The reason why we cannot know if or when we ever reach this point is that, as in a kaleidoscope, the various factors concerned are changing all the time—factors such as the amount of capital, the level of skill and inventive capacity, and the ever-varying relations of international trade. If, therefore, we waited until there were either more or fewer people to enquire whether we had reached our goal before the change, we should find—as in the game of croquet in *Alice in Wonderland*—that some, if not all, the factors concerned would also have changed in the meantime. What we can say is that, so long as the average standard of living is rising, we cannot from the economic point of view either be greatly over- or under-populated.

There are countries now, however, and there have been times in this country, in which we can be quite sure that there are either too many or too few people relatively to their economic situation. Take India, for instance, with its high birth-rate and its small amount of capital per head, the great density of its people and the primitive methods of its agriculture. There we know that there are already too many people for a sufficiently high standard of living, and that every improvement in social conditions tends to be cancelled out by an increase in population resulting from a fall in the death-rate. Australia, on the other hand, we know to be under-populated, since it is unable to develop its industry on the mass-production lines it would like, owing to the small number both of workers and consumers it contains (see Chapter 23). But as for this country, if we were a few millions more or less, what difference would it make from the economic point of view? As I suggested, in dealing with the economic consequences of a declining population, the right answer has to take so many different factors into account that we just cannot know what it is. But we do know that a big change either way, i.e. a rapid decline or increase, would be bad, as it would be so difficult to make the necessary adjustments. If we could increase the birth-rate tomorrow by a wave of a wand up to 25 or 30 per thousand, we should be terribly embarrassed. It would make the food and housing situation worse, and emphasise the shortage of maternity beds, midwives and teachers. The new torrents of children would be even worse placed than are those of today with regard to the number of schools, equipment and clothes. Similarly, a rapid decline would lead to an inconveniently drastic reduction in all the goods and services consumed by mothers and children.

Even if we cannot answer the economic puzzle, however, can we solve the social one, which was referred to in trying to estimate the probable consequences of population decline?

> "Too many folk in London city,
> It isn't a joke,
> It's almost a pity!"

Many of us would wish to echo Eleanor Farjeon's nursery rhyme when we are in a traffic jam or trying to enter a tube or bus at rush hours; or being jostled off the pavement outside Charing Cross; or if there should be a return of the pre-war queues of the unemployed, or when new rashes of buildings spread over the countryside. But we can take heart. None of these evils is necessarily a sign or a concomitant of too big a population. Unemployment I have shown not to be due to there being too many people, but to faulty organisation of industry, which the experts concerned say can to a very great extent be avoided. Similarly, traffic difficulties and the unregulated spread of buildings over the countryside and in the town can also be avoided by proper planning. According to the Report of the Scott Committee on Land Utilisation in Rural Areas (1942), only 11·3 per cent of the land in England and Wales is covered by buildings, roads, railways and other forms of the works of man. Even if all houses were to be built not more than twelve to the acre—and in most big towns a far higher density of building is sure to take place—according to Sir Raymond Unwin only 2½ per cent of the land need be occupied by buildings.

We must therefore look at the puzzle of what should be our ideal numbers and pass on, realising always that as regards the next generation at any rate, those who will be parents are already born, and before the war were definitely fewer in number than their own parents. Therefore any increase in the population in the next generation is a virtual impossibility, and *what we have to avoid is starting on the toboggan run of a continuing decline, the consequences of which we can only with difficulty imagine.*

THE TIME-TABLE

It would perhaps be generally agreed that we should aim at a birth-rate which would stabilise the population at not much less than its present level and enable it to remain stationary as regards numbers, and stable in its age composition. Should it go down more than a very few millions in the meantime, we should then have to try to increase it from the level it would have reached by that time. We must ask, therefore, how many years we can allow before our goal is reached. A population policy might aim at achieving its goal at once, or it might plan for a rise to take place over any given number of years. At the present moment, as the result of a high birth-rate in the war years, the net reproduction rate is over 1, and if, as is expected, the birth-rate remains high for another two or three years, may well remain over 1 for that time. This would only be a cause for congratulation if housing conditions could be rapidly and substantially improved, educational plans carried out and our economic situation improved.

However, once the present shortage problems have been solved, the sooner we can obtain a population which will keep stationary as regards numbers and stable in its age composition, the better. The later the time by which the birth-rate necessary for this purpose has been achieved and stabilised, the higher will be the proportion of people past child-bearing age at that date, and the larger the number of aged dependents. To redress the balance at that time would necessitate a larger average family and a higher burden of child dependency than would have been the case if the birth-rate could have been raised earlier. The transition period aimed at, therefore, should be the shortest possible compatible with the need for providing the material and social conditions in which parents might be asked to have more children. This might take from ten to fifteen years. At any rate, the change-over from the small- to the medium-family pattern should have taken place within thirty years, when the population of England and Wales is likely to be 3–5 millions less than today. Otherwise things may well have gone too far to be reparable without efforts so great as to be unlikely to succeed.

I have already pointed out more than once that the numbers of those who will be parents in the next generation will be fewer than the numbers of their own parents, leaving immigration out of account. If, then, the size of the average family continues to remain only about two, each new generation must and will have fewer children to reach the productive ages in their turn than we have now. Even if during the next few years, as a result of war and post-war conditions, we manage to maintain a net reproduction rate of 1 or more for two or three years, it is highly unlikely it would be maintained for longer owing to the anticipated inevitable decline in the numbers of marriages due to there being fewer people of marriageable age.

We must therefore go forward to try to increase the average size of the family as fast and as hard as we can, knowing, as is pointed out above, that a falling population in a few years' time seems inevitable and that the chances of an increased population are negligible for the next generation at least. Even the chances of a stationary population thirty years hence are by no means too bright at present. Everything depends on the success and wisdom of the psychological and practical policies for a bigger average family, which may be adopted. And it must never be forgotten that these can necessarily only take effect at long range, since additional births today can only produce an additional set of parents twenty or thirty years hence. Therefore the sooner we start the more likely we are to be successful.

THE SIZE OF FAMILIES REQUIRED FOR A STATIONARY POPULATION

Those who put in a plea for larger families are often accused of wanting a return to the Victorian family of ten or more children. It is important, therefore, to know what is the family size necessary to maintain a stationary population. I have already shown that for some time past in this country between 85 and 90 per cent of women have married before they are 50. This high proportion of married women means that in order to achieve a stationary population it would only be necessary for each married couple to have on an average about 2½ children—instead of the average of about 2 they have today. (The ambiguity in these figures is due to there having been no satisfactory statistics to show the exact numbers.) Supposing we step up this average to 3, we should then allow (1) for families who are unable or unwilling to have any children, or more than one or two, and (2) for the small proportion of births (about 6 per thousand) which are illegitimate. This proportion is likely to become less as contraceptive technique becomes more widely known and more effective.

How should this average of three children be attained? Is it more desirable that, as far as possible, families should be of nearly equal size? Or is it more desirable to have a wider spread, including a fair proportion of both small and large families? In Sweden it is families of equal sizes which are being encouraged—since it is thought that equality in this respect will help to promote equality of living conditions and of the responsibilities of citizenship.

According to Swedish computations, an average family of three would necessitate nearly two-thirds of the families having four children, and at least 15 per cent more than four. Cattell, on the other hand, thinks that only 25 per cent of the families need be as high as four.

The American writer on eugenics, Frederick Osborn, advocates a greater variety in family size than do the Swedes. He points out that though the one-child family is everywhere admitted to be a mistake, a considerable proportion of parents never will wish to have more than two children. There are, however, a certain number of parents who have a special love for children and would both enjoy a large and noisy family and be able to afford it. He would therefore like to see family sizes vary between two and six or seven. This is what is in practice likely to happen in this country if we succeed in attaining the higher birth-rate we need.

Chapter 14

POPULATION POLICIES—GENERAL PRINCIPLES

"Great things must be done greatly—
With a great purpose, a great courage,
A great energy and a great persistence."
Elizabeth Barrett Browning.

THE MEANING OF A POPULATION POLICY

THE very complexity of the causes which underlie changes in population trends, as also their multiplicity, make it imperative that the policies designed to encourage or to change these trends should in their turn be correspondingly complex and varied.

When the question is asked, "What is meant by a population 'policy'?" we realise that there can be few actions, whether political, economic or social, taken by any Government which do not, in fact, influence the number of children parents may want to have, the number of young men and women who marry, the numbers who die at different ages or of those who enter or leave the country for the purposes of migration. But such actions do not necessarily represent a series of policies, since in the past they have usually been designed for other ends. But now, with our present trends, it is essential that the Government and public opinion should never fail to take the population aspect of any action into account, in order that actions which may be harmful to population trends may be avoided as much as possible and vice versa.

It is, for instance, unquestionable that recent legislation on education, national insurance, national health and family allowances will probably help to affect the birth-rate in an upward direction, though none of these had been planned, at least to any great extent, with the birth-rate in view. On the other hand, recent happenings, such as the apparent disregard of the needs of large families in the lack of provision of sufficient large houses at rents which the lower-paid workers with several children can pay, the taking away of marriage and children's allowances from men in the Forces, the encouragement of emigration to the Dominions of young people—all of which are bound to have a discouraging effect on the birth-rate—seem to have been decided on without enough consideration of their undesirable results in this direction.

A population policy, then, must be deliberate, and must consist of "the conscious and systematic application of measures designed to influence the course of population change in socially desirable directions." * Even if we consider, therefore, under this heading only those measures which are aimed at changing either our death-, migration- or birth-rates, an effective population policy will be nearly as "wide and deep as our national life itself." On what principles should these measures be based?

THE DEATH-RATE

To take first the death-rate. Here our policy must inevitably aim, as it always has done, at saving life and postponing death as long as possible. But as has already been shown when discussing future trends, even if the growth of medical knowledge and better conditions succeed ultimately in eliminating all deaths under the age of 80, this could do little to ensure eventually a stationary or rising population. For already the proportion of those today who die before their child-bearing age is over is very small, and to postpone

* F. Lafitte.

the arrival of death for the elderly would obviously have little effect on the numbers of future generations. There is still, on the other hand, considerable room for the reduction of still-births and abortions, and of the death-rate among infants in the lower-income groups. This must obviously be achieved by better housing and town planning, better medical care, higher standards of living and so forth.

MIGRATION

It has been shown that during the present generation the movements, whether in or out of this country, have been small. A population policy may well be directed towards attracting certain categories of valuable citizens from among nationals of countries who can be readily assimilated, and at the same time towards refraining from giving assistance to too many of the young and strong among our own people who may wish to leave this country. But the encouragement of immigration on a really large scale would indeed be a counsel of despair, since it would show that as a nation we have valued our national ideals and way of life so little that we have not done enough to encourage or to help our own people to maintain their own numbers.

THE BIRTH-RATE

It is in policies affecting the birth-rate, then, that we may most hope that something really effective may be done. The steady drop in the size of the average family per married couple during the last three or four generations has brought about our present anxiety. Little can be achieved by encouraging marriage either at an earlier age or among more people, since, as has already been shown, earlier marriage does not necessarily mean larger families, and the number of those now marrying in this country is about as high as it can be—being about 90 per cent of those of marriageable age. Unwanted childlessness must, of course, with medical assistance be reduced to its very minimum, and scientific research to this end be encouraged.

MEANS OF RAISING THE BIRTH-RATE

The really important issues are: first, how to strengthen the wish for more children among the great majority of potential parents; and secondly, how to facilitate the carrying out of this wish. The great goal, therefore, to which population policies must be directed is so to educate and so to help those who are young parents today, or who will become mothers and fathers during the next thirty years, that they may have, not the one- or two-child family typical of the present generation, but a medium-sized family at least sufficient to maintain a stationary population.

(1) *Changes in the General Conditions of Life*

What should these changes be? First and foremost, young married people must have confidence in the future, and must feel that successive Governments will be capable of tackling adequately the immense problems which face this country and—in co-operation with other countries—those which face the world.

These problems are not likely to be solved for some considerable time to come, and doubts as to ultimate solutions are difficult to avoid. But if young people feel a sense of direction, of high purpose and of wise leadership, they may be able to hope that devastating wars will not recur, and that life can be led without fear of their shadow; also that—through wise planning and action on the part of our Governments—mass unemployment will not again raise its ugly head.

During the last few generations the great majority of our people have experienced rising standards of living—higher wages, more leisure and improved social services, and they must feel hopeful that this progress will continue. It is interesting to note, however, that there are those who see signs that the very anxieties with respect to public affairs are leading some young parents to have more children than they might otherwise have done, so as to compensate by a rich family life for present discontents with regard to the harsh world outside.

The importance of standards of living continuing to improve is not always realised. For, although the achievement of any given reform demanded by our standards of today may remove some contemporary obstruction to parenthood *at the time it is brought in,* the probably higher standards of a later generation will demand ever greater resources to satisfy them. Once, for instance, enough houses have been built up to our present standards to remove the handicap their lack causes to a higher birth-rate, houses of a still higher standard will begin to be asked for; and the provision at that time of houses up to today's standard will no longer give the necessary stimulus. Today we are asking for one bedroom for two children; in twenty years' time we may be demanding that each child shall have its own bedroom; and if this cannot be provided, parents will then still put forward overcrowding as a reason for not having more children.

This, though true in general, and of very great importance in considering policies for the future, will not hold in cases where the standards have already reached the maximum practically possible. This will, in due course, probably be the case as regards certain parts of the education and health services. But what we can most likely expect in general in this country is that the standards of the middle classes of today will become those of the working classes tomorrow; and that with these standards will be associated the shrinking from the discomfort, drudgery and responsibilities associated with the care of children which is so marked a feature among many young married couples in the middle classes today. Accompanying, therefore, any policies which are directed to improving economic and social conditions, and of even more urgent importance, should be educational campaigns directed towards a change of values, a greater robustness of outlook and simpler ways of living. Otherwise the desire for leisure, comfort and luxury will be apt, as generation succeeds generation, to continue to frustrate or overwhelm any desire for more children.

(2) *Attitude of the Government*

In this book there is not space to embark on any discussions on fundamental changes in our economic and political systems which, to some, still seem necessary before confidence in the future can be obtained. Nor to suggest whether this should be achieved by nationalisation, by private enterprise controlled in the interests of the community or by a combination of the two.

However our industrial or political system may be modified, it is essential as a condition of a permanently higher birth-rate that Governments should realise the urgent importance of population problems and the complexity of their causes, and "should be prepared to show that neither dilatoriness nor lack of conviction shall stand in the way of securing the survival of the community"* they represent. Governments must, indeed, show that they are prepared resolutely to carry out

* F. Lafitte.

every reasonable kind of policy—educational, psychological, economic or social—which will help convince people that their children will be wanted and cherished by the country as a whole, and that their own sacrifices on behalf of their children will be shared by the community.

(3) The Individual's Attitude to Life

Perhaps the most important condition of all is an increase of faith in life itself on the part of young parents-to-be, so that sufficient zest and a sufficient sense of purpose should be found among them. Even if they have experienced war, they have not experienced unemployment, and there are, we know, many potential parents who are already prepared to have more children, provided material and economic difficulties are removed or reduced. But in addition there are at least a proportion of parents who, being fearful, irresolute and defeatist as regards life itself, need to be encouraged to show the necessary courage and optimism, whether this is based on religion or inspired by humanitarian ideals, or both. Parents who are thus afraid of life are found in all sections of the population—mainly perhaps among the more intellectual and sensitive. They are probably not typical, but the contribution of children they might make cannot be spared.

A DOUBLE THREAD

What is necessary, therefore, is that our population policy should consist of a double thread. *It must seek first through education, through changed standards of value stimulated by a religious or philosophic faith, to encourage the love of children and the desire for a family bigger than the present one- or two-child type. This is essential, and already those who really want*

*children often sweep difficulties and obstructions away
as unimportant. But the difficulties and obstructions are
real, and so the second thread must therefore consist—
as far as possible—of their removal and mitigation. In
this way a material environment can be created which
—combined with a more robust faith in life—should
make it possible to bring up families of children sufficient in number for a rich family life and for a stationary
population without undue sacrifice on the part of the
parents.*

THE PRINCIPLES OF A POPULATION POLICY

There are certain principles which alone are con-
sistent with the standard of values of a democratic
community and so must be observed in this country.

The voluntary nature of parenthood has pride of
place. Our children must be wanted children. The control of conception has got so sure a hold already in this
country that it is too late, even if it were desirable, for
it to be uprooted. Emphatically, this would not be
desirable. Public opinion has already shown itself to
be overwhelmingly in favour of accepting the control
or spacing of births necessary to the planned family.
It has always been found, both in this and in other
countries, that where there is lack of information as to
reliable methods of contraception, useless or harmful
methods are used instead. The provision of information
on scientific methods of birth-control should therefore
form an integral part of the public health system of
the country, and more research as to better methods
should be encouraged.

*Next, these children—born when and where they are
wanted—must be of good quality.* Parents who are
likely to be able to establish a satisfactory home life
for several children should be encouraged to have the

children they desire. But parents whose children are likely to suffer from hereditary defects, or who are themselves subnormal mentally, physically or morally, should be expected to refrain from having children. In addition, in order to avoid any waste of the children who are born, child welfare and other services should be further developed, so that the children we have may be saved from premature death or privation.

Thirdly, the possession of children should not demand too great a sacrifice from the parents of their other occupations, interests or leisure. This is particularly true in the case of the mothers, since motherhood absorbs so large a proportion of their energies. Any conflict which may arise between the desire for life and interests outside the home and the demands of parenthood within it must be resolved by making the rearing of a family a more efficient and at the same time less arduous task than in the past. In the following chapter I will endeavour to show how these principles can be carried out in practice.

Fourthly, reforms proposed as part of a population policy must contribute towards the welfare of the whole population.

Chapter 15

POLICIES TO INFLUENCE PUBLIC OPINION 1

PROPAGANDA AND EDUCATION (ADULTS)

I HAVE now examined, however inadequately, the more important of the strands which make up public opinion as regards population issues, and the more important psychological causes why parents wish to maintain the small-family pattern. Most of the latter can be grouped under four main headings:

(1) The lack of a sufficient sense of social responsibility, so that the interests and pleasures of the individual, whether as a parent or taxpayer, overshadow in his mind the needs of the community.

(2) The lack of sufficient spirit to face courageously the risks and anxieties of life, inseparable from bringing up several children.

(3) The lack of appreciation on the part of potential parents of the delight and interests offered by a larger family as compensation for the work and sacrifice it involves.

(4) The lack of knowledge of the technique of rearing several children well.

ON THE PART OF THE STATE

The State cannot, at this juncture, stand idly by, any more than it could in war-time when the very existence of the community was threatened. "Propaganda" may not be a popular conception, but it merges into education when it gives the truth with regard to the facts of the situation and their interpretation, and when it appeals to the reason as well as to the emotions. Education prepares the citizen to play his part and maintain the standards of life of the community in which he is born. In this sense it includes all the influences to this end which can be brought to bear on the individual from the cradle to the grave. Let us enquire in particular how these can be used to develop first a sense of social responsibility, and next an understanding of the values of family life. The influence must be considered of the home, the school, the youth organisation, the university, the adult class, the Press, the radio and the film. We have to take into account both the parents of today, most of whom have completed their formal education, and the children and young people who will be the parents of tomorrow.

The primary aim of education to these ends, whether of adults or children, must be to encourage high ethical standards and a re-orientation of values which would lead both to a keener sense of the responsibilities of citizenship in general, and to a greater realisation of the importance of the life of the family group. I suggested earlier that during the war, the feeling of responsibility for the nation was easy to arouse, and millions of men and women were prepared to sacrifice everything, even life itself, so that the nation might survive when faced with dangers from outside. A similar concern for the community must be ensured in the equally serious situation arising out of our population trends which threaten the nation with a gradual shrinkage and disintegration from within. *Parents must be asked, not to have children for the State, but to realise that having children, though primarily their own affair, is by no means only their affair, since the first concern of any community is its own survival.*

THE PRESS AND THE B.B.C.

It is unlikely that in this country it will ever be considered right that directives of any kind, on however important a subject, should in peace-time be issued either to the Press or to the B.B.C. Even during the war, the main work of influencing public opinion was done mainly through the willing co-operation with the Government of the newspapers and of the B.B.C., who united voluntarily to stress the importance of the war effort and of a courageous outlook. Once, therefore, the Government has decided on the policies it proposes to adopt in order to prevent too great a decline in the population, there is every reason to hope that the same kind of co-operation will be once again maintained.

The Press already plays a big part in education for citizenship and has shown a distinct interest in population issues. And there is little doubt but that it will continue to do so as long as the subject in its turn arouses interest among the general public. Women's journals and the women's pages in the general Press are of particular importance, in that they can call the attention of their readers to the fundamental issues behind individual home and family problems and make the idea of a large average family familiar. For instance, the *News Chronicle* consistently assumes a family of four children.

The B.B.C. is in much the same position as the Press; that is to say, it tends to follow rather than to lead public interest. Responsibilities of citizenship are often discussed and, once the attention of the nation has been aroused, it will no doubt develop regular programmes of discussions and talks relating to family questions and family life. Already before the war, some discussions and some individual talks on these subjects were arranged, and recently several discussions on family life have been staged. But so far not a great deal has been done. If, as is probable, the Royal Commission on Population adopts a definite point of view and makes many positive recommendations, the B.B.C. is likely to play an important part in popularising its findings.

BOOKS AND PAMPHLETS

Books and pamphlets are of obvious importance. Books on citizenship and handbooks dealing with the technique of home-making and child-care threaten to become a spate. But much less has been written on problems of population. Novels are of particular importance in this connection. Victorian stories of attractive large families have probably aroused the envy of many members of the small-family groups of today—I well remember my own delight in Charlotte Yonge's *The Daisy Chain*—but today most stories, plays and even advertisements take the small-family pattern for granted.

FILMS

The use of the film for education on population and family issues could also become of the greatest value. The facts can be made attractive and easily understood by means of diagrams and pictures. Films can also be used in connection with education in child-care, home-making and many different problems of family life, whether such films are shown in the ordinary picture-houses or to schools, colleges and organisations of all kinds by private projectors.

A far greater influence, however, would be the appearance in the ordinary commercial film of stories about large families. Films such as *The Sullivans* or *Little Women* have been immensely popular. But in most films where children appear, it is usually the only

P.B.—6

child who is featured. Unfortunately the British film
industry is handicapped by regulations which limit
seriously the employment in the preparation of a film
of children under 14. It is virtually impossible, therefore, to depict in a British-produced film a happy home
life with several children. This problem needs to be
solved.

INFORMATION SERVICE

It is much to be hoped that the different Ministries
concerned with social services affecting family life, such
as the Ministry of Health, the Ministry of Education,
the Ministry of Town and Country Planning, the
Ministry of Food, will provide teaching material—
pamphlets, exhibitions, photographs, films or posters
on population questions, etc., through their Public
Relations Departments. It would be best of all, perhaps,
if a particular Ministry, new or old, were to be given
the continuing duty of collecting information on, and
conducting research into, all aspects of the population
problem. It could indeed fill a far more ambitious
function. It could survey the whole field of Government action in the light of its probable effect on
population trends, and could make suggestions as to
what new policies should be carried out, whether to
influence the numbers of the population or its quality.

FORMAL AND INFORMAL METHODS OF ADULT EDUCATION

With the 1944 Education Act, adult education stands
on the threshold of new developments. The demand for
discussions, talks and classes will probably increase—
owing partly to habits formed in the Forces, and partly
to the undoubted increase of interest in public questions
since the war. Classes or discussion groups in any of
the social studies help to give some understanding of

society and the citizen's responsibilities towards it which inevitably include population issues. For instance, discussions on philosophy and ethics may do much to help the individual formulate his faith and social purpose, and attain to higher standards of personal behaviour both as a citizen and in his family relationships. Some knowledge of simple biology, hygiene and psychology should help him understand his own body and mind, and the physical and psychological relationships involved in marriage and child-rearing.

Technical courses on the arts and skills connected with the home, such as budgeting, hygiene, food values, dressmaking, laundry and child-care are of particular importance.

On the physical side of child welfare a great deal of education has been assimilated by parents during the last forty or fifty years. But there is still, as is testified by the infant mortality figures, a large number of parents among the less responsible or less intelligent sections of the population whose children would greatly benefit if they would accept teaching of this kind.

As I pointed out earlier, when discussing why parents did not want more children, wiser methods of child management and of housekeeping would make the task of looking after children a far easier and pleasanter one than is often now the case. It is only for a few that I would advocate child psychology as it is often taught, since half-understood Freudianism may well lead in some cases to an increased lack of confidence on the part of the semi-intellectual parents. One of the greatest present needs in this connection is for the training of many more lecturers able to put across in a common-sense way simple psychological truths which mean something to the ordinary parent.

It is highly satisfactory that the Ministry of Education

has recently issued a circular urging local education authorities to make increased provision of classes of every kind in home-making and child-care.

Courses on The Family or Family Relationships, such as are being held in London, at Morley College and some evening institutes, are valuable for helping those who are endeavouring to establish a good home-life. There may be some who think that such a course would involve an undesirable exposure of intimate family affairs. Experience shows, however, that many of the problems which seem to a given individual to be peculiar to him or his family are, in fact, shared by others; and that objective discussions on such problems form a first step to their solution.

EDUCATION OF THE PARENTS IN THE HOME

A great deal of education in child-care is carried on by those who are naturally in contact with the mother and sometimes with the father in the home. These include teachers, school-attendance officers, doctors, health visitors and nurses, who meet parents in connection with the welfare of their children. How best to give this informal training is the task of the various professions concerned. In the same way the different kinds of centres for mothers and babies, or for child- or marriage-guidance, have all a part to play and are already making a valuable contribution. Organisations such as the Women's Institutes, Women's Co-operative Guilds, Townswomen's Guilds and so on, once they appreciate the need, can arrange demonstrations, talks and discussion groups and film shows on facts with regard to population and family problems and the need for larger families.

Chapter 16

POLICIES TO INFLUENCE PUBLIC OPINION 2

EDUCATION FOR CITIZENSHIP AND FAMILY LIVING IN SCHOOLS

(i) EDUCATION FOR CITIZENSHIP

HOW are we to carry out in our schools both education for citizenship—the most important aspect of which is the development of a sense of social responsibility—and education for becoming a good and responsible member of a family group?

The new Education Act is big with promise to facilitate better education for all by raising the school-leaving age, by providing for smaller classes, better buildings and equipment and so forth. But even more important than such administrative questions is the need to bring about a change in the content of education—in what is actually taught. School-teaching is still concentrated to a great extent on the education of the individual as an individual. Since the child's chance of success in life depends so much on his vocational training, and since the range of his leisure-time interests is determined so much by the cultural training he receives, it is perhaps not surprising that the curriculum in our schools has in the past mainly concentrated on these; so that the child's social education—his relationships with the communities of which he forms part—has been, comparatively speaking, neglected.

How different is this conception from that of Plato! He defined education as "that training in virtue from youth up which makes a man passionately desire to be a perfect citizen, knowing how to rule and how to obey

with justice. This, I think, is that for which we alone
should reserve the name of education, regarding the
training which aims at wealth or some bodily strength,
or any other accomplishment apart from reason or
justice, as mechanical and illiberal and entirely unde-
serving of the name!" The need to develop a feeling
of responsibility both for the nation and for smaller
groups must therefore be increasingly stressed in our
schools. It must be taught through many different subjects in the classroom, gained through contact with fine
individuals and experimented with in practice in the
daily life of the school and in service to the community
outside. Most good schools already succeed in arousing
a sense of loyalty to themselves. But the need to influence a boy or girl to transfer this loyalty when he
or she leaves school to the town, the country or the
world is less generally recognised. It must be deliberately encouraged in schools through contacts with the
neighbourhood and with the conditions of life—social
and political—in this country today, and through
knowledge of its great achievements in the past and
of its present ideals.

Training in Standards of Value

The most fundamental task of education is to help
boys and girls as they grow older to develop, through
their religious training, through the life of the school
and otherwise, a feeling of purpose and high standards
of value as regards personal, family and public affairs.
Not that young people, while still immature, are capable
of achieving a clear-cut philosophy of life, since this
baffles many of their seniors. But discussions on matters
of conduct will help some of them at any rate to realise
that in both personal and social behaviour principles
and standards of value are involved, and will aid them

to lead happier and more useful and purposeful individual lives.

Knowledge of the Modern World

In order to learn to care about the community and to feel some responsibility for it, children must get to know all they can about its ways. While still of primary-school age, the child can become acquainted with his own town and neighbourhood and, through local surveys and by "interviewing" those who carry on the affairs of the town, can begin to learn something of the way in which it works. The older boy and girl can forge in imagination the link between the life of the neighbourhood and that of the nation; and will be able to study the economic and social structure of the country and the world both through existing subjects on the curriculum, through the addition of new courses in simple descriptive economics and politics, and through informal discussions, films, plays, etc., in or outside the classroom.

Though most schools give lip-service to education for citizenship, there are still not a large proportion—especially of grammar schools—which give their children any real opportunity for knowing and for thinking clearly about the community around them and about contemporary public affairs. The Ministry of Education has so far done very little to foster this aspect of education. I myself have frequently asked groups of young people in the Forces—coming from all sorts of schools—how many of them had learned anything about contemporary society and the citizen's responsibilities towards it while at school. The proportion who had done so was consistently only one in seven! And yet without such education, how can parents be expected as citizens to have been sufficiently accustomed to think of the needs of the community to consider these a factor of any importance when determining the size of their own family?

(ii) EDUCATION FOR FAMILY LIVING

Education for family living, like education for citizenship, is also many-sided. It must encourage an appreciation of the fundamental values and happiness of family life. It must consider how to develop the best kind of relationship between different members of a family and to show how these relationships change with the changing years. It must include sex education and the technique of running a home and of bringing up children. It has, therefore, moral, psychological, biological and technical aspects.

In the nursery, infant and primary schools every opportunity should be given for children to understand the importance of home-life. The children can compare their own lives with those of children of other countries or in other parts of their own country and in other times. They can learn something about how houses are built, their equipment, the various public services affecting a home and how its material needs are met. They can learn unselfish ways and how to help look after younger children. This is especially important for the large proportion of children who are themselves members of very small families. On the other hand, children in larger families must be protected, if possible, from overmuch domesticity.

Sex Education

As regards sex education, so much has recently been written that it need be treated here only very briefly. It used to be taken for granted that sex education should be given by parents; and, when well done, this is certainly the ideal way. But for the ordinary parent it is a very difficult task. He or she frequently does not know the right age at which to tackle the different aspects of such teaching for a particular child, and may not even have the right vocabulary.

In the primary school, however, some understanding of the physical facts of reproduction can come in as part of natural history, or can be given by any wise teacher in answer to incidental questions. When described simply and without fuss, the facts as regards the structure of sex throughout the animal kingdom are accepted without difficulty by the normal child. For older children, biology should be universally taught, and should include human physiology and reproduction and matters connected with the quality and quantity of the population. More important still, an effort must be made to show young people as they are growing up the value of good sex relationships, and to promote higher ethical standards with regard to these than prevail today. Sex education must give young people the feeling of the dignity and worth of the human body and of the importance of considering the well-being of others where sex relationships are concerned.

During adolescence it is vitally important for young people to understand something also of the working of their own minds and how to think clearly and without prejudice. Early adolescence also is the period in which changes—physical, emotional and intellectual—take place with startling rapidity, when boys or girls are emerging from dependence on their parents, when they begin to question their own family's ways of living and when strains may arise which embitter family life. These can be minimised if boys and girls are led to understand that these new physical feelings and emotions are not unique to them, but are characteristic of their particular stage of development.

As they approach adulthood, their interest begins to shift from their parents' homes to their own rôle as future husbands, wives and parents. It is at this stage, perhaps, that they can most fruitfully consider the ethical standards as regards sex relationships which were referred to above. Not that these are easy to define, since we are probably in a transitional period in which standards are changing in many respects. Young people will to some extent have to find out for themselves which of the values their parents held are abidingly true and which need to be adapted in response to social change.

The following extract from *The Needs of Youth in Our Time** sums up far better than could be done by the present writer what education for family living should consist of and what it might achieve:

"Young men and young women who had been prepared for adult living in the other respects we have described could hardly have avoided developing an understanding of the social value of homes and families, of the institution of marriage and of the responsibilities which attend it. The health knowledge referred to will also be of use to them as members of homes and families and when they come to found homes and families of their own. The young woman should have acquired, in addition, a sound knowledge of the major practical arts involved in the management of a home. She should have received a good grounding in cookery and dietetics, in marketing and budgeting, in first-aid and home nursing, and in carrying out simple household repairs. The young

* A Report issued by the Scottish Board of Education, 1946.

man should be familiar with the principles of dietetics and have obtained some practical ability in the simpler forms of cookery.

"He should know how to administer first-aid and how to make himself handy about the house, and, like the young woman, he should have learned the sensible handling of money for both personal and family purposes. The young woman should know how to look after her health and prepare her home when a baby is expected and how to care for and train a baby. The young man should have enough knowledge of the woman's part in parenthood to enable him to treat her with sympathy and understanding.

"Both sexes should have learned through the example of their own upbringing and from their general education that it is essential for those who have the care of wives or husbands and of children to give some study to how that care may best be exercised. All the aspects of their preparation and development—physical, mental, moral and spiritual —should have combined to give them a healthy, knowledgeable and respectful attitude to sex and reproduction. They should view it in the proportion appropriate to their stage of development. That is to say, they should not be so knowledgeable as to have nothing left to learn and no discoveries to make, but they should be informed enough to enable them to avoid both the troubles and disasters which are apt to attend upon sexual ignorance; effects which arise from regarding sex as a shameful mystery to fly from or to snigger furtively over. The sense of mystery properly attaching to sex in the minds of healthy young men and women is that which sur-rounds it as a source of inspiration and aspiration of poetry, art and music, of tenderness, devotion and sacrifice, and as the means by which life is continued and developed."

At present our schools fall far short of satisfying these requirements. In the boys' grammar schools they have been virtually ignored, and only a small proportion of girls' grammar schools attempt a little housecraft—and then usually for a minority of their less intelligent pupils. Many of the modern secondary schools have, as pre-Butler Act senior schools, indeed done their best, but have been handicapped by the low age of their pupils.

Before leaving the question of schools, I would like to refer to two perennial problems:

(1) Should there be a Different Curriculum for Boys and Girls?

The first problem is whether there should be a different curriculum for girls and for boys, in view of the fact that about 90 per cent of girls will marry and have to run homes of their own. When the first secondary schools for girls were started some two or three generations ago it was of urgent importance to show that girls could reach as high an intellectual standard as boys in most of their school subjects, and could proceed to universities and enter occupations previously closed to them. On the establishment of this equality the development of opportunities for the education of girls seemed to rest.

So far, therefore, few distinctions between the curriculum of girls and boys have been made. In the pre-war senior schools girls usually took domestic subjects, while boys did woodwork. In the grammar schools girls have often paid more attention to the arts—English literature, modern languages, and history and music—

while boys have paid more attention to classics, mathematics and physical sciences. But that is about all.

In 1923, when the Consultative Committee of the Board of Education considered this problem, they pointed out that "all children have to be educated with two ends in view: (1) to earn their own living, and (2) to be useful citizens, while girls have also (3) to be prepared to be makers of homes. Boys and girls should be educated on similar lines, although not necessarily at the same pace, so far as concerns the first and second aims. As regards the third aim, which is special to girls, we consider that *some definite preparation should be given during school-time*. This is particularly necessary at the present time because the requisite training tends to be given less and less in the home. The influence of the university has to some extent been harmful, inasmuch as the curriculum of secondary schools has been largely planned to meet the requirements of the comparatively few pupils who desire to proceed to the university and has ignored the needs of a large proportion of girls who approach life through other avenues." The report also adds that "there will be some gain in efficiency if the girl associates the arts relating to her home with the thoroughness and intelligence required in other subjects. There is a gain too in her feeling that her teachers appreciate the importance of home duties and have full sympathy with her development in this direction." *

The report proceeds to show, however, that since a very large proportion of women undertake paid work before they marry, and that those who do not marry have usually to continue with it through the whole of their lives (while those who do marry may wish to return

* *Differentiation of Curricula between the Sexes in Secondary Schools*, H.M. Stationery Office.

to it), girls must be educated for some paid occupation as well as for family life.

Here, then is a dilemma. Girls must continue to be prepared for careers outside the home. Yet it must be recognised that family life will absorb the main energies of the overwhelming proportion of them, and that to make a home and to bring up a family well needs a very high standard of skill, understanding and technique. The educational psychologists of today hold the view that any general "training of the mind" by school subjects does not in fact happen, but when particular skills and aptitudes are learnt they can only be applied to other subjects under certain definite conditions, which include similarity of content and a consciousness of the need for such application.

It follows, therefore, with regard to home-making that the knowledge and skills required should be given to girls when still at school. There is a balance to be redressed, and their education must be modified so as to prepare them to a far greater extent than at present for their lives as home-makers and mothers. The age at which such teaching should be given must be carefully chosen. Teachers have told me that the interest of girls in small children tends to come at the beginning of puberty, but puberty itself comes at different ages in different individuals. For younger girls child-care is probably best taught through other subjects, such as biology, homecraft and hygiene; but for all older girls there should be compulsory classes both in child-care and homecraft. Technicalities may well be forgotten in later years; but what is important is for girls to become familiar with small children and to learn the right attitude towards them. In these days of small families many a girl hardly sees a baby at home—let alone handles one. It is not surprising that many women now dread the idea of having a child, since they feel they would not know how to look after it.

Not that this training should be limited to girls only. Much connected with the care of the home, sex education and the bringing up of children, as we pointed out before, should be taught to boys as well as to girls. Neither, conversely, should girls with a special bent be prevented from becoming skilled in what so far have been considered as boys' occupations, such as engineering.

Perhaps the solution will be found in the fact that much of the curriculum in our secondary schools is still largely based on tradition and needs drastic reconsideration. It is hoped that in the near future new types of school curriculum will be worked out better adapted to the needs of growing boys and girls than anything that has been known in the past. This applies particularly to grammar schools, where many of the subjects today are taught more as watered-down university courses rather than as material which can be used to help children understand more about the world around them, both now and as a preparation for their adult lives.

(2) Co-education and a Mixed Staff

Difficulties which may arise between men and women are often due to a lack of opportunity, when young, of mutual companionship and knowledge of the interests and characteristics of the other sex. This is particularly important for those who, as so often happens today, are either only children or come from a family of only girls or only boys. If the sexes, while at school, learn to respect and understand one another and to work and play together, this should provide the most appropriate kind of preparation for an harmonious family life, while the very differences between them should enrich the life of the school. The desirability of this should go far to outweigh any administrative problems which co-education may bring.

Even when co-education among pupils may be considered impracticable, it is all the more important that the staffs of all schools—especially those for older boys and girls—should contain members of both sexes. Not only would this tend as a rule to a more normal type of society among the members of the staff themselves, but it would also enable boys and girls to learn to know well and to respect adults of the other sex outside their own family. The new Education Act has prohibited the exclusion of married women teachers, and this should ensure that the importance of a good family life will be much more stressed than at present. In girls' schools now it is the career outside the home rather than in it which is usually presented by the staff as the most important object for ambition.

FUNCTION OF THE SECONDARY SCHOOL

There are many who suggest that education for citizenship and for family living should be left mainly to the county college and to youth and adult organisations. I should like, however, to put in a plea here that the main responsibility should be taken by the secondary school, which will soon be keeping all young people until they are 16 and a higher proportion than at present till they are 18.

It will be quite impossible in the county college in the bare seven and a half hours a week for which each young person will attend to deal with any but a few of the many vitally important subjects with which their education should be concerned. There are many educationists who advocate that part of the precious seven and a half hours should be given to vocational training. In any case, how can the needs of physical and health education, of the arts, citizenship and family living *all* find a place? In some county colleges citizenship and family living may be offered, but even then there will be time for but few of their varied aspects. Youth organisations are at present attended by not much more than half the young people; and those who do attend them find at their disposal an even greater multiplicity of interests and shorter hours in which to carry them on than they will at the county college. Since, however, the responsibilities of citizenship and family living should not be regarded as the interests of the few, but are the inescapable responsibilities of all, at least a foundation with regard to them needs to be given in the secondary schools through which all children must pass during their formative years.

(iii) Young People Between Fourteen and Eighteen Outside School

Boys and girls at work have greater experience of the world than have those in school, and on that account are often more ready to be interested in social questions. They often have more contact with the other sex and are more subject to sex stimulation owing, at least in towns, to the social life and recreation offered to them. How can they be so influenced that they may become responsible citizens and have a healthy and happy attitude to marriage and family life? Education to these ends in clubs, evening institutes and county colleges must be of every kind—moral, intellectual and practical. Where classes are held, social questions and ethics must be studied. But the informal methods are likely to be more effective. The easy talk in discussion groups round the fire, the local survey, the documentary film, the drama, the newspaper, books and pamphlets, are all valuable for this purpose.

Responsible citizenship is probably best encouraged, as in schools, through the way of life of club or college itself. The more self-government there can be within appropriate and clearly defined limits, the more co-operation is sought between all those concerned, the more is the sense of social responsibility likely to emerge. But to be a good member of a club or college is not enough. Young people must be brought into direct contact with the wider community mainly through service of some kind.

Classes in the domestic arts and in many matters relating to the proper running of a home and family, and to the relation between the home and the public services should be provided for both boys and girls.

It is at this stage, too, that sex education begins to be most fruitful. In many organisations today, experiments in sex education are being conscientiously tried. The difficulties with regard to their extension lie, not in the biological aspects, but in determining standards of value where sex questions are concerned. As Dr. Macalister Brew says: "The great gap in sex education evidences itself at that very age when boys and girls become interested in each other. There is a general tendency to lock up one's information on sexual function into a separate compartment and not to realise how such knowledge may affect one's behaviour. The remark 'Yes, we know all that, but they don't really think we can behave in that way' is too frequent to be ignored."

As for topics such as the care of children, home nursing and the equipment and running of the home, perhaps the best time to deal with them by youth organisations is in "engagement classes," which have been successfully started in some youth clubs, and which catch the young man and woman just when they are really interested in marriage, in home-keeping and children. Much more might also be done than at present for those who are already married: classes might be arranged at a time when a young mother can leave her home; and the imperative need for the young father to train for his share should not be forgotten.

A real problem exists in the difficulty of providing effective moral training, especially for the large proportion of those who come from homes which have no religious creed and who are frequently without a moral anchor of any kind. One of the main educational problems at this juncture is how to help these to attain high standards of value based on the fellowship of man. So far, the task has hardly been attempted, but the more experiments can be carried on for this purpose, the better.

As I have already pointed out, however, nearly half of our young people do not belong to any sort of organised body at all, though this situation will be drastically changed when the county colleges have got going. For them, as for adults, it is the printed word, the radio and the film which have most influence.

(iv) THE TRAINING OF TEACHERS

The adequacy of all the proposals made with regard to education will be conditioned by the quality of our teachers, present and future, and by the way in which they are trained to carry out the kind of educational work proposed in this chapter. In most training courses for teachers of older children stress is today laid on subjects in which the student intends to become a specialist. This is particularly true of the university student. A re-orientation of training courses is therefore called for, so that all teachers in training may have the opportunity—whether through formal courses, discussion groups or practical activities—to acquire some knowledge of philosophy, sociology, politics and economics, and of biology, so as to help them understand the different kinds of societies and of family groups in which they and the children they will teach have to live.

It is not suggested that all teachers should become specialists either in social studies in general or in "family living" in particular. But it is essential, for the sake of their own development, that knowledge on these subjects should be acquired after school age, when they are themselves sufficiently mature to understand the issues. Moreover, as has been pointed out in connection with schools, education for citizenship and for family life depends, not only on formal teaching, but also on indirect allusions, individual contacts and personal example. Teachers who are themselves good citizens and happy members of their own families, or who at any rate appreciate the importance of both these sides of life, are essential if high standards in these matters are to be conveyed to the children they teach.

It may be objected that the teachers' training course leaves no time for additional subjects. But it must be remembered that not only is an additional training year confidently anticipated, but that the demands from the schools, both secondary and primary, are likely to be considerably changed in the future. The schools will be likely to devote far more attention to helping the child understand the communities in which he lives and the situations he is likely to meet in real life. It is essential, therefore, that the training of teachers should be prepared and adapted to meet this development.

Refresher Courses

A great deal more must be done to help the teacher on the job who has not had the benefit of training of this kind in his student days. The Ministry of Education should follow up its pamphlet on Sex Education with other suggestions for education in citizenship and for family living. More conferences and summer schools dealing with methods of teaching both social studies and various aspects of family living should be arranged by local education authorities and by the various organisations concerned.

(v) UNIVERSITY EDUCATION

The influence that our universities might have on public opinion with regard to matters of urgent national importance such as those we have been discussing is very great. They are concerned with a highly selected body of young people who form the intellectual élite of the population, and who are training for professions such as teaching, the church, medicine, industry and journalism, where they will be in a position to guide and stimulate public opinion. The universities provide an intellectual discipline to prepare these young people for their separate vocations. They should also help them gain a philosophy of life and a standard of values.

As centres of research they aim at the discovery of fresh knowledge and new relationships with regard to the problems with which we are concerned. They thus have immense opportunities. There are a mass of unsettled questions in demography, education, psychology and biology, solutions of which are urgently required in order to help the country formulate population policies based on knowledge rather than on guesswork. At present the subjects chosen for research frequently do not appear to be selected on account of their intrinsic importance. They are often frivolous in relation to the urgent need for enlightenment in so many of the problems which have baffled the shattered world of today. At any rate, while these problems remain unsolved, research should be directed far more than it is now to social, psychological and biological studies. This should eventually have an immense cumulative effect on our national destinies.

With regard to the teaching of students, universities even more than the schools have so far concentrated almost entirely on the interests, vocational or cultural, of the student as an individual, and have not considered his education as a member of society—whether of the State or of his family—to be their responsibility. Since social relationships of these kinds will have to be entered into by *all* students, while any given vocational need or cultural interest is inevitably the concern of a section only of the student body, it is essential that the function and responsibility of universities with regard to social education should be more widely appreciated.

Here also the knowledge likely to help a student become a responsible citizen and a good member of a family should be drawn from Philosophy and Ethics, the Social Studies, and Biology and Psychology. But we are up against a dilemma. The proportion of students specialising in any of the above subjects will in all probability remain a minority only, at any rate for a very long time. The practical problem is how to modify the curriculum for specialists in other subjects to enable them to be trained for what are the common responsibilities of all. As it is, the more a student concentrates on his own subject, the less it is possible for him to be educated for life as a whole. Specialisation must continue for many students in preparation for their vocations. Should not, however, the balance be redressed and provision made during the three or four years a student stays at the university for the inclusion of courses to help him understand the society in which he lives and his responsibilities towards it?

Many proposals have been put forward as to how this might be achieved both for students taking vocational and cultural courses. In vocational courses they can be given some knowledge of the social, economic and political aspects of society which provide the background for any occupation. Cultural courses could stress more closely than at present the applications of their subjects to society and human welfare. More Final Honours Courses than at present might include two or three subjects, of which one at least could be one of the social sciences or philosophy.

Lastly, there might be adapted to the conditions of British universities some form of the Survey Courses in the social and natural sciences respectively, such as have become familiar in many American universities and which provide the basis for a general education for all students before more specialised work begins.

Chapter 17

ECONOMIC ASSISTANCE FOR PARENTHOOD 1

FINANCIAL

"The neediest are our neighbours if we give heed to them,
Prisoners in the dungeon, the poor in the cottage
Charged with a crew of children, and with a landlord's rent,
What they win by their spinning to make their porridge with
    milk and meal to satisfy the babes,
This they must spend on the rent of their houses
Aye, and themselves suffer with hunger,
With woe in winter rising a-nights
In the narrow room to rock the cradle,
Carding, combing, clouting, washing, rubbing, winding,
    peeling rushes.

Pitiful it is to read the cottage-woman's woe,
Aye, and many another that puts a good face on it,
Ashamed to beg, ashamed to let neighbours know
All that they need, noontide and evening.
Many the children, and nought but a man's hand
To clothe and feed them; and few pennies come in
And many mouths to eat the pennies up."

    "Piers Plowman," by William Langland, 1330–1400.

IT will be generally agreed that where the wish for a child is present, the main single factor accounting for the small-family pattern today is the economic one. "I can't afford another baby" is the usual phrase. And in all social classes except the very richest, the starting of a family or the addition of a child usually involves standards of living lower than would otherwise be the case. Among the poorer income groups it tends to plunge the whole family into poverty; among the better off of the working classes and in the middle classes it means the sacrifice of amenities. The nature of the sacrifice involved varies obviously according to the income group concerned and the circumstances of the individual family.

The refusal to have another child on account of the economic handicap it represents is, as has already been suggested, by no means necessarily a selfish one. It is found perhaps most often among those parents who wish to give their children the best possible education and start in life. They would prefer to have one or two children for whom they can do everything they think necessary, rather than several to whom they would have to give only a more meagre upbringing.

In such cases no propaganda or educational campaign is likely to succeed in arousing a desire for a larger family *unless the community shows quite definitely that it is prepared vigorously to help remove or at any rate to reduce as many as possible of the financial obstructions to parenthood.* The help given must be ungrudging and generous, so as to make it crystal-clear that the community wants children, and is prepared to share the cost of their upbringing with their parents.

I have already acknowledged the need for greater economic security all round, and for the attainment of the various higher standards desired by those living at different income levels respectively. But to solve this last problem we are concerned not only with absolute standards of living but also with the relative differences in these standards arising from the size of the family. Supposing we raise the incomes all round of a given economic group, either as a result of an increased production of goods and services, or of an increased share of the national income which is devoted to earnings. Valuable as this would be in order to encourage general confidence, it could do nothing in itself to solve the problem of the comparative additional expense to the family and lowered standard of living which would be caused by the birth of a child.

What, then, is the nature of the economic provision for children which the State can reasonably be called upon to make? There are various possible forms of help. Some have already been established, others are still to come. The problem must be looked upon as a whole, as it is a matter, not so much of principle, but rather one of tradition or of administrative convenience as to which of the possible forms such provision should take.

These forms of assistance can be grouped as follows:

(1) *Assistance by Money Grants*

This would include such provisions as family allowances, scholarships and bursaries, dependants' allowances and maternity benefit.

(2) *Rebates on Account of Children*

This would include children's income tax rebates, children's rent rebates and rebates with respect to cost of travel, etc.

(3) *Subsidies and Price-control*

This would include subsidies such as are now given for milk for mothers and children; and for flour, bread, meat and other necessary foodstuffs, the benefits from which accrue mostly to larger families. It would include also the production on utility lines, with maximum prices, of goods used by children, such as perambulators, cots and clothing.

RELATIONS WITH THE SOCIAL SERVICES

There are certain services which can be provided much more efficiently and satisfactorily by the community than by the individual. These include: (1) *The Educational Services*—including the provision of schools of all types, school meals and amenities, and an extended school medical service. (2) *The Health Services*, which under the National Health Service Act will cover all the health needs of the population, including the special services for mothers and babies.

The discussions which have sometimes arisen as to whether cash allowances or social services are the better form of provision for children largely miss the point—for, emphatically, *both are necessary*. They are supplementary to one another and not alternatives. Services such as those for education and health—if they are to give equal opportunities to all children and be available for all classes of the community—must be provided by the State. The great bulk of the people in this or any country have never been able to afford to buy them, so where they are not provided by the community, they do not exist at all for the greater part of the population. This is generally conceded. It is in regard to such matters as school meals or clothes, which have in the past been provided by individual parents, that controversy arises. It is pointed out by those who advocate assistance in kind that the provision of certain commodities or services by the State is more economical, since they can be provided more cheaply in bulk than if bought for each separate home. The State can thus make use of all the economies of production on a large scale. It can also often make any assistance it gives kill two birds with one stone, as, for instance, when milk was given at a cheap rate in schools, both to safeguard the health of the children and to encourage the prosperity of agriculture. Drawbacks of a cash allowance are that money ostensibly provided for children may not necessarily be spent on them by the neglectful type of parent, whereas they are bound to benefit by the social services, and that allowances can, by those who disapprove of them, be represented as "a bribe to parenthood."

The protagonists of cash allowances, on the other hand, maintain that these are far simpler to administer than provision in kind, that they strengthen the family as an institution and enhance the responsibility of the parents by placing the onus for wise spending on them. It is further pointed out that each child has individual needs which are best known to its own parents and many of which can only be supplied in its own home. Some services, moreover, can be provided at lower cost in the home than through public social services. Take the case of school meals. It is true that the food can be purchased in bulk by the education authorities. But considerable sums have to be paid for administration, labour and fuel, which duplicate much of what is being done in the home, since the average mother gives unpaid labour and is—in a large proportion of cases—already preparing meals for other members of the family. It was stated by Sir John Anderson, in the debate on the Family Allowances Bill, that the cost of administration of school meals will take £20 millions out of the £60 millions school meals will cost for the 75 per cent of the children who it is estimated will want them.

The suggestion that cash allowances constitute a money bribe is an easy jibe, which would only be justified if allowances combined with social services were on so large a scale that child-rearing would become a profit-making affair. This is not contemplated by anybody. They are indeed designed to contribute to the economic needs of a child—not to pay for the services of the parents.

The policy to aim at in this country is to ensure that taken together—cash allowances, tax or rent rebates, subsidies, controlled prices and social services—the various forms of provision should cover the essential subsistence needs of children. These needs—adequate food, house-room, clothing, education, recreation and health—are fundamentally the same for all children. But those who are accustomed to spend more than this minimum on their children for certain services will, unless they are well off, in all probability still wish to restrict their families, so that they may provide for them services and goods of a standard higher than those offered by the State. This problem will have to be met, and I return to it later. These parents are a minority, and will become fewer as the State provision attains nearer and nearer to the best that could possibly be provided. Both the Education and the National Health Service Acts bear witness to the principle that the country is aiming at giving every child what best suits its individual needs; in some aspects of education and health this is already being done. The same principle must be applied later to the provision of the other needs of childhood.

FAMILY ALLOWANCES

Let us start by considering the various forms of financial assistance, and begin with the most important of these—family allowances.

Until recently the case for family allowances was based, not so much on the need for more children, as on justice being done to the children who are there, and on adequate provision being made for them. Eleanor Rathbone—the great protagonist for family allowances —always put forward as the strongest reason for their establishment the fact that the mothers and children of the community by virtue of their very existence had a moral claim on its resources irrespective of the earnings of their husbands and fathers.

Equally important was the argument that the large amount of poverty existing before the war was especially marked among the children of the poorer large families. Although only 3·9 per cent of the families were estimated by Rowntree in 1936 as having more than three children, these included more than a quarter of the child population. In every social survey made since the 1914 war the same conclusions were arrived at, viz. that a large percentage of families with children were living in primary poverty on incomes which, however wisely spent, failed to provide for the bare necessities of healthy existence. Thus, in 1934, Sir John Orr made his famous estimate that 25 per cent of children under 14 years of age in England and Wales lived in families where the money available for food averaged only 4s. per head per week—a sum which at the prevailing level of prices could only buy food "insufficient in every constituent necessary for health." Rowntree showed in 1936 that in York 53·5 per cent of working-class children in any one year were born into poverty, while nearly half those between 5 and 15 lived continually in poverty. As for those whose fathers were in low-paid employments, he estimated that nearly 90 per cent lived in poverty for over five years of their lives. Children living in these homes were inevitably under-nourished. Ten times as many were under the standard height and four times as many below the standard weight as compared with children of the better-off classes. It has already been shown that the infant death-rate among the poorer classes is considerably higher than that among the rich. The bad results on the health of the mother in such families and her premature ageing through strain are also notorious.

Moreover, before the war there were many industries —in some of which the wages were fixed by Trade Boards —which paid less than the amount Rowntree considered the barest minimum for the support of a husband and wife and three children. Since the beginning of the war average earnings have risen by over 50 per cent, but there has been a considerable increase in the cost of living. The proportion of children in the larger families still living in poverty, though less than before, must therefore still be substantial.

It was when alarm first began to be felt with regard to our population trends that the possibility of family allowances serving as a real encouragement to parenthood was eagerly canvassed by Eleanor Rathbone and others. It was felt that a good family allowance scheme would demonstrate, perhaps more than any other measure, the community's resolve to enter into partnership with parents.

EXISTING FAMILY ALLOWANCE SCHEMES

Until 1946 the State had given children's allowances to men in the Forces as part of their pay, and to unemployed men, to widows, to men under the Workmen's Compensation Act, and to destitute persons as part of their benefits or assistance. These allowances varied in amount under the different schemes, but none of them was apparently related to any scientific estimate of the cost of child maintenance. Now they have mostly been swept away and the parents of all dependent children after the first receive 5s. per week under the Family Allowances Act of 1945. It will be remembered that the allowance is paid up to the compulsory school-leaving age or so long as the child is under 16 and is full-time at school or is apprenticed. First children receive an allowance of 7s. 6d. only if they are children of widows, unemployed or sick men under the National Insurance Act, or of workers under the Industrial Injuries Act.

EXISTING SCHEMES AND THE BIRTH-RATE

To what extent are these allowances, as they are, likely to serve as an encouragement to a higher birth-rate? "Not at all" is the probable answer. The rate of 5s. per child under the Family Allowances Act is too low to represent any appreciable addition to the family income; and in the case of widows, the unemployed, etc., since the new allowances are to be substituted for and not added to the old ones, the change involves the most paltry increases. As for men in the Forces, although their basic rate of pay has been increased, they are receiving much less in the form of general family allowances than they did from their former special children's allowances.

The present schemes can at best do nothing more than mitigate the poverty of the low-income groups. Even when the universal free school meals provided for under the Education Act eventually materialise, which will not be for several years, these two forms of provision together cannot by any stretch of the imagination be expected to stimulate the birth-rate—except perhaps for those who may be so much on the margin of financial doubt as to whether to have a child that it will take very little to push them over.

TYPE OF FAMILY ALLOWANCE SCHEME REQUIRED

What conditions should a family allowance scheme fulfil in order that it may form a useful part of a population policy?

(1) *The Rate must be Adequate in Amount*

How can this be reckoned? The following table showing the cost of child maintenance was worked out by
Lord Beveridge in his Report on Social Insurance, on
the basis of 1938 prices. It takes no account of rent, and
it assumes that the average value of school meals and
milk at that time was only 1*s.* per week per child, since
the numbers of those being fed were, at that time, so few.

Table 13.— The Cost of Child Maintenance

AGE OF CHILD	AVERAGE EXPENDITURE ON				
	FOOD	CLOTHING	FUEL, LIGHT	TOTAL	AVERAGE
	s. d.	*s. d.*	*s. d.*	*s. d.*	*s. d.*
0–5	4 6	0 7	0 3	5 4	
5–10	6 0	0 10	0 3	7 1	7 0
10–14	7 0	1 1	0 3	8 3	
14–18	7 6	1 3	0 3	9 0	

Beveridge estimated that the rise of prices that had
taken place since 1938 would justify an average allowance of 8*s.* per week, which at present prices would be
nearer 10*s.* Moreover, as I pointed out before, it will be
many years before universal school meals materialise,
and even then it is assumed that they will only be
taken by three-quarters of the children, and probably only during the 200 or so school days there are
in any one year.

Since the cost of living is more likely to increase than
to go down, it is essential that *family allowances should
be increased as soon as possible from the present level
of 5s. to that of 10s., and that they should be subse-
quently adjusted periodically to changes in the level of
prices.*

(2) *Should the Scheme start with the First Child?*

This is not easy to answer. There are probably few
families in the country which cannot support at least

one child adequately, and, as I have already shown, there are few parents who are not prepared to have one or two children and for whom economic incentives are therefore unnecessary. In relatively few cases indeed is expenditure due to one child likely to result in the fall of the family standard of living. This will be all the more true when the financial burden of parenthood is further lightened through the extension of public services in connection with education and health from which first children cannot be excluded. The cost of any scheme, if the first dependent child is excluded, is, moreover, more than halved.

On the other hand, it is often the first step in starting a family which is economically the most difficult to take. The birth of the first child necessitates not only all fresh equipment—pram, cot, clothing, etc.—but also means that those mothers who have kept up paid work after marriage will have to give it up. An allowance for the first child, therefore, might do much to reduce the gap between marriage and the child's birth. Not that childbirth at an earlier age can in itself change the small-family pattern, but it may well prevent the stereotyping of a way of life without children. Where parents wish to have a larger family, an earlier start would give them more time in which to do so with adequate spacing of the children desired.

(3) Should Allowances be Graded?

(a) According to the Place in the Family.—The importance of encouraging the birth of children after the first two is paramount. It would therefore be more effective for this purpose to increase financial assistance for children after the first two through higher rates of benefit. Family allowances in France increase considerably with the place of the child in the family, as do those in the U.S.S.R., which do not indeed start until the fourth child.

(b) *According to the Age of the Child.*—The needs of children increase rapidly with age. Lord Beveridge is strongly in favour of allowances being graded accordingly. This is already the case in Unemployment Assistance as follows: under 5 years old the rate is 7s. 6d.; between 5 and 10 years it is 9s. 6d.; between 11 and 15, 10s. 6d. and between 16 and 21, 12s. 6d. It would be a great advantage if family allowances could be graded in the same way.

(c) *According to the Parents' Income.*—Any flat-rate family allowance scheme could at best only cover, together with the social services, the minimum cost of a child, and is not likely to do much to encourage the birth of children among those income groups who are accustomed to spend more on their children than the minimum, and whose contribution to the next generation, partly for this very reason, tends to be the lowest of all. As the social services increase—both as regards their scope and standard—the additional amount any parents, with however high a standard, would wish to spend on their children is likely to become less. At present, however, higher income groups in fact do spend much more on their children than do the lower, and yet their birth-rate trends are the lowest. It would, nevertheless, be neither politically desirable nor practicable to suggest different rates of family allowances for those in different income groups. The establishment of additional voluntary schemes, on the other hand, may well be encouraged in different occupations. Special schemes have already been adopted by most of our universities, by the big banks, by the Wesleyan ministry, and among the Church of England clergy in many dioceses. In most cases these are paid for by the employing bodies. But they could also be financed by voluntary insurance, which would constitute a horizontal redistribution of income among those in the same income group, so that the childless contributed towards the children of others.

There is thus a great deal to be said against the flat-rate system, which ignores differences of age and order of the child in the family, if not of the income of the parents. But the advantage of simplicity in administration speaks eloquently in its favour. This system has now been adopted in the Family Allowances Act, and only experience will show whether it will be considered desirable to change later.

CHILDREN'S REBATES ON THE INCOME TAX

Perhaps the most effective and fairest way of helping better-off parents is through children's rebates in connection with income tax, which have been allowed for many years and implement the principle of taxing people according to what they can bear. It is clear that a man with dependent children is less able to pay income tax than a man with no children. Up to now the amount of income from which rebates are deducted has been a definite sum, which is at present £60 for each dependent child. This form of tax relief can, of course, apply in its entirety only to those whose incomes are sufficiently high to allow for children's rebates to be deducted after all other rebates on earned income, on a wife or as a personal allowance have been taken into account. A rebate on a fixed amount of income has, therefore, two disadvantages: it can be of little or no use to those with very small incomes, while for those with a large income it permits of too little difference between those with and without children. A far fairer form of rebate would be one which, like the rebate on earned income, is based on a specific proportion of the total income. This would no doubt necessitate a "ceiling" in order that those with really large incomes should not be having more tax deducted than the cost of bringing up a child. An appropriate proportion for children's tax rebates might be 10 per cent of the income, with perhaps a ceiling of £150 on which rebates may be allowed.

CHILDREN'S RENT REBATES

Provision for housing subsidies to be given in the form of children's rent rebates was first included in the 1930 Housing and Slum Clearance Act in order to try to solve the dilemma of providing adequate housing accommodation for families with several children. It is just these families who now can least afford to pay the rent required for a large enough house and who live under the most overcrowded conditions. The regulations under the 1930 Act laid down the principle that rent-relief "should be given only to those who need it and only for so long as they need it," and expressly empowered local authorities to charge differential rents to tenants. Later the permission to use the subsidies as a pool to enable rents to be fixed according to the varying needs of tenants was extended to houses built under all the other Acts. It was mainly with the needs of families with children in mind that this principle was laid down. If children's rent rebates were to be adopted everywhere, the poorer families with several dependent children could occupy the larger houses, which it is now impossible for them to do. The figures show that overcrowding grows steadily worse as families increase in size. In Great Britain only one hundred and twelve local housing authorities have adopted this system of rebates, difficulties having arisen in some places through the rebates being accompanied by an income test, which was resented. But just as family allowances are given to families irrespective of their income, so might the same principle be adopted in the case of children's rent rebates. This is all the more desirable, since the 5s. per child provided under the Family Allowances Act is only about half the minimum sum required at the present cost of living for keeping a child without any allowance for rent.

It is much to be hoped that the allowance of children's rent rebates will be imposed as a statutory obligation on local housing authorities, so that they will be bound to use at least part of the grants they receive for subsidies as a pool out of which children's rent rebates can be given.

It is difficult to think of how children's rent rebates could be allowed in houses belonging to private landlords. It has been suggested that the local authorities might give subsidies which would ensure that a move by people with families into a larger house would not involve the payment of any more rent. But as a large proportion of working-class houses are already publicly owned, and as a still larger proportion will be publicly owned in the future, the adoption of children's rent rebates, even if only in council houses, will go far to enable the larger families of children to be suitably housed.

SCHOLARSHIPS AND BURSARIES

(1) Schools

Under the 1944 Education Act there is a considerable extension of the power of local education authorities to give maintenance grants or other financial assistance to children who need help in order to enable them to take part in school activities, such as school journeys, or towards fees and expenses of those who attend schools at which fees are payable; or who are over the compulsory school-leaving age. These grants will be a valuable supplement to the present rate of family allowances, provided that the local authorities are sufficiently generous in the interpretation of their powers.

(2) *Universities and Training Colleges*

The number and scale of university scholarships has also been substantially increased under the Act, and they can now cover the whole cost of university education. Fees in training colleges for teachers have been abolished. All these concessions will be of considerable importance as a reassurance to parents who want to give their intellectually able children the best possible education.

MATERNITY BENEFITS AND ALLOWANCES

Under the new National Insurance Act a very considerable advance has been made with regard to maternity benefits. Instead of the former grant of £2 that a married woman could claim on her husband's insurance, and on her own, she will now be able to receive a maternity grant of £4 on either her husband's insurance or on her own. Since most married women are not in paid occupations, this definitely constitutes an advance. As in the future all medical services in connection with confinements will be free of charge, the grant of £4 will be available to cover some at least of the equipment required for the new baby. Later it may be desirable for this sum to be increased. In addition, for non-employed women there is an attendance allowance of £1 per week for four weeks, and for an employed woman a maternity allowance of 36s. a week for thirteen weeks, beginning about six weeks before her confinement is expected, provided that she abstains from work. A better arrangement would be if she could continue to receive her pay. Although it would be impossible at this stage to impose this obligation on private employers—and it would probably militate against the employment of married women—there is much to be said for its being adopted by public authorities, such as the Civil Service and local government authorities.

CHILDREN AND NATIONAL INSURANCE

The position of widows has certainly been improved under the National Insurance Act, and in future they will receive 26s. a week (instead of the former pension of 10s.), together with 7s. 6d. for the first child. Subsequent children receive 5s. under the Family Allowances Act. But the proposed allowances for children are not nearly enough for widows without other resources—who are the great majority—and will frequently have to be supplemented by the assistance authority. The same applies to the children of men who are unemployed or ill. It is much to be hoped, therefore, that allowances for children under both Acts will be considerably raised in order that parents may know before they embark on a family that whatever happens to the father, the economic welfare of the children will be safeguarded as a right by the community.

MARRIAGE BONUS

A marriage bonus might perhaps be paid, not so as to encourage marriage—since the rate is already high— but in order that young people may set up house and furnish without the present drag on their resources caused by the hire-purchase system. It often happens that the financial obligation imposed by hire-purchase payments causes parenthood to be postponed.

SUBSIDIES AND PRICE-CONTROL

During the war, in spite of many privations and strains, the health of mothers and children reached a new high record. This was largely due to the fact that rationing arrangements enabled them to receive milk and other important foodstuffs on a priority basis, and that subsidies on foodstuffs—combined with higher earnings and a great increase in school meals—enabled children as a whole to be better fed than they had ever been before. It is important, so long as food and milk shortages remain, that these priorities should be retained. It is desirable, too, that subsidies for the kinds of food most necessary for children should also be retained if, without subsidies, they would be beyond the reach of the poorer parents.

As to goods required by children other than food, such as cots, perambulators and clothing, their production on a utility basis with fixed conditions as to quality and price has enabled them to be purchased without too great a sacrifice. It is in this case also desirable that the arrangements and controls should be kept in being.

Chapter 18

ECONOMIC ASSISTANCE FOR PARENTHOOD 2

SOCIAL SERVICES FOR MOTHERS AND CHILDREN

ADVICE ON BIRTH-CONTROL

IN discussing the principles which should underlie policies for encouraging the birth-rate, I took the view that it is essential that parenthood should be voluntary, and that information on good and effective methods of birth-control should be made available for all women. If this could be achieved, nearly all children would be wanted children, the use of ineffective methods and harmful practices such as abortion would be minimised, and suitable spacing between births would prevent the exhaustion of the mother or the neglect of the children.

At present local health authorities are only permitted to arrange for information on birth-control to be given to married women for whom "pregnancy would be detrimental to health." There are some humane doctors at the maternity and child-welfare centres of various kinds, who stretch this phrase to cover cases where another child would plunge the whole family into greater poverty. But arrangements for providing any kind of contraceptive information by local health authorities are by no means universal: only about 240 health authorities have either established special clinics or made arrangements with voluntary clinics, hospitals or individual doctors for the purpose.

There are, however, few women who come for advice on birth-control who are not in need of advice on other health matters as well. What is required, then, is not so much clinics specifically for information on methods of birth-control only, but rather general gynæcological centres—as proposed many years ago by the late Chief Medical Officer of the Ministry of Health, Sir George Newman, who suggested the establishment of centres where mothers could get advice, not only on birth-control, but for sterility and for any trouble which may have arisen in connection with child-bearing.

It may well be that if researches now being undertaken produce foolproof and effective forms of contraceptives, no special advice on birth-control itself will eventually be needed; but the need for general advice will always remain. Mothers' Centres of these kinds, therefore, should be widespread and should provide appropriate advice for fathers as well. There are other services which some of these centres might very usefully render. A certain number of conscientious young people, coming from families where there is some kind of hereditary defect or tendency to defect, want advice as to whether they ought to marry, or if married as to whether they ought to have children. More doctors should be trained to give this advice. With regard to advice on sterility, only a handful of clinics have as yet been established. Here again is urgent scope for a widespread service. Those which have been started have already proved their usefulness; moreover, if a larger number of potential parents came for advice in this connection, it would enable more rapid progress to be made in research as to the causes of sterility.

ANTE-NATAL CARE

The importance for mothers and their babies of antenatal care and of medical services of the highest quality during and after confinement, is now appreciated. But although it has been recognised in theory for at least a generation, it has as yet by no means been everywhere satisfactorily carried out. Although deaths in childbirth have fallen during the last twenty years from over 4 to under 2 per thousand, this has been largely due to the conquest of puerperal fever by better nutrition and by the use of the sulphonamide drugs. But during the same period, although the general infant death-rate has fallen to 43 per thousand, deaths under one month, which are mainly due to premature births and pre-natal troubles, have only diminished by about 10 per cent, and still-births are still so numerous that they equal nearly two-thirds of the infant death-rate.

The proportion of still-births and of deaths of infants during the first four weeks has been found to be much higher among mothers who have had inadequate care and poor diet than among those living under better conditions. In 1941 a report was published in Toronto which showed that "in a low-diet group of four hundred expectant mothers, there occurred 8 per cent premature births, 6 per cent miscarriages and 3 per cent still-births, while in the supplemented food diet group only 2·2 per cent premature births and no miscarriages and still-births were recorded. The average duration of labour in the supplemented diet group was shortened by five hours."

Since 1937 milk has been provided at half-price for expectant and nursing mothers and children under 5 and has been given free to those with less than a certain income. During the war this service was extended, and now includes also the giving of vitamin tablets, fruit juice and cod-liver oil with marked beneficial effects. Both our maternal mortality and infant death-rates have reached new low records during and since the war.

Today about three-quarters of the mothers of babies

born attend an ante-natal clinic, though this proportion varies enormously from place to place and especially between town and country. The clinics are found by no means everywhere, and great variety exists also in the efficiency of their arrangements.

This difference between the services provided in different localities is largely due to the fact that the great majority of the provisions of the Maternity and Child Welfare Act of 1918 under which services for mothers and children have, up to the present, been provided are permissive only and not imposed as a statutory obligation. It is therefore a good augury that the National Health Service Act, in placing the responsibility for maternity and child welfare services on counties and county boroughs, has made most of them statutory in character.

THE CONFINEMENT

It has been shown that the maternal death-rate had fallen to under 2 per thousand births in 1942, though for many years before 1930 the rate had remained obstinately round about 4 per thousand. The famous report on Maternal Mortality published by the Ministry of Health in 1930 pointed out that at least half these deaths were preventable and asked the question, "If preventable, why not prevented?" The problem has now been largely solved by greater medical care and more medical knowledge. When the standard of services given by the best authorities is made compulsory everywhere, the lowest rates known today should become universal.

Here also the statutory provision to be made under the National Health Service Act will mark a new chapter in the care of mothers. Midwives attend about two-thirds of all confinements, and about half the midwives today are in the public midwifery service. Since their training in maternity work is longer and more specialised than is that of doctors, in this respect they are better qualified than is the doctor for attending normal births when the home conditions are good. Better-off women who are confined in their own homes prefer being attended by a doctor; but in recent years there has been an increasing proportion of women, now about 50 per cent, who are confined in hospital or maternity homes—priority being given in the case of public hospitals to first births or abnormal cases.

What is required, and what the National Health Service Act will in fact provide, is that in normal cases every mother will have the aid in her own home of an efficient midwife trained in the use of anæsthetics and with specialist assistance available. Where the case is abnormal or home conditions are not suitable, hospital accommodation and services will be available. At present the supply of hospital beds is much smaller than the demand, and needs to be substantially increased.

CARE OF INFANTS

The care of infants has improved to such an extent since the beginning of the century that, as was pointed out above, the death-rate is only one-quarter of what it was at that time. There are, however, wide variations "between social classes, and these have become more marked as the child grows older and is more affected by home surroundings. Even in 1942, the total deaths of infants of 1–12 months exceeded by more than one-third the middle-class figures of twenty years ago." A report of Birmingham University on conditions just before the war showed that "babies whose families were on the means test standard had a mortality risk of 150. If their fathers were getting unskilled wages, their risk was over 100. If the fathers were well-to-do, the risk was 23·1."

Health Visitors

Since 1906 a fine service of health visitors has grown up, and their number and qualifications have steadily improved. "The functions of the health visitor are mainly preventive and educational. She must be able to pass on her knowledge and inspire confidence. . . . Her responsibility extends to expectant and nursing mothers, as well as to infants and children under 5. As visitor to the homes of families and a member of the Welfare Centre staff, she links the home to the clinic and is the farthest outpost of the Child Health Services. . . . The Health Visitor Service has done marvels, but today most health visitors have a thousand or even more children under 5 under their care, and as a result, visits—particularly after the first year—are somewhat infrequent." * The numbers of health visitors must therefore be considerably increased.

The Infant Welfare Centre

The infant welfare centre is too well known to need description. There are now almost 4,000 in England and Wales, and in 1944 nearly three-quarters of all babies born alive were taken to a centre at least once. The trouble comes after the first year, as many mothers are not convinced as to the need for taking their toddlers, amongst whom in consequence improvement in health has been much less than in the case of infants. The result is that far too many children under 5 enter school with preventable complaints. The establishment of more nursery schools and classes would do much to help in this respect.

* P.E.P. Planning No. 244.

DOMESTIC ASSISTANCE

The need to prevent the overwork of mothers with several young children is a crying one. Local authorities already have the power to provide home-helps for mothers who are ill, or who are confined at home, and also during pregnancy where conditions make it desirable. The duties of a home-help are confined to domestic help and the care of the other children and do not include nursing. A charge of anything from 7s. to 30s. per week according to income is made. Up to the present the service has been on a very small scale, as during the war it has been extremely difficult to find enough of the right kind of women. It needs to be widely extended.

THE FUTURE

It is fortunately no longer necessary to lay down what in theory a satisfactory health service for mothers and babies should include, since the new National Health Service legislation will bring all the necessary services within its scope. These services as they affect the mother have been summed up officially as follows:

"Maternity and Child Welfare and Midwifery.—The Act makes it the duty of every local health authority to make arrangements for the care of expectant and nursing mothers and of children under 5 years of age who are not attending school, and who are therefore not covered by the school health service. Their arrangements will include ante-natal clinics for the care of expectant mothers, post-natal and child clinics, the provision of such things as cod-liver oil, fruit juices and other dietary supplements, and in particular a priority dental service for expectant and nursing mothers and young children. . . .

"The local health authorities are made responsible for a complete midwifery service for mothers who are confined at home . . . the midwife will have the usual right—and duty—to call in a suitably qualified doctor in case of need.

"Mothers who for any reason have their confinements in a hospital or maternity home will be in the care of the hospital and specialist service. It will also be the object of that service to provide locally for all specialist, obstetric or gynæcological care which may be needed.

"*Health Visiting and Home Nursing.*—It is made the duty of the local health authority to provide for a full health visitor service for all who are sick or expectant mothers, or those with the care of young children. This widens the present conception of health visiting into a more general service of advice to households where there is sickness or where help of a preventive character may be needed. It is also made the duty of the local health authority to provide a home nursing service.

"*Domestic Help.*—Under the existing law, local authorities are empowered to provide home-helps as part of their maternity and child welfare functions, and the Act extends this to cover the provision of domestic help to any household in which it is needed on grounds of ill-health, maternity, age or the welfare of children for an appropriate charge."

CARE OF SMALL CHILDREN

It has been urged that the objection on the part of young mothers to being tied all day and every day to their children is very natural and that provision must be made to solve the problem. A big step forward will be made under the new Education Act under which nursery schools are to be established wherever desired by the mothers. These can be attended by children between 2 and 5 for several hours in the day, and give the midday meal.

For children under 5, whose mothers do not want them to go to the nursery school, there should be more day nurseries on the lines of the war-time nurseries, prepared to take children when the mother is out at work. A home-keeping mother may also want relief for a short period in the day only. Local health authorities are already empowered to run nurseries, or they might be undertaken, as in Edinburgh, by voluntary organisations. Before the war there were several nurseries in Edinburgh open for two hours only every morning to give the mother at home much-needed relief. Very few of such nurseries should be open to children under 2, since not only is the staffing required for under-twos very expensive to provide, but it is generally agreed that they are usually better off and run far less chance of infection in the familiar surroundings of their own homes.

There are many mothers who will either not be within reach of a nursery—as these are unlikely to be started in less densely populated neighbourhoods—or who fear the dangers of infection. Small groups of mothers living in a given street or block of buildings might well make arrangements among themselves or through a tenants' or community association. There might also be a Home Service Scheme such as was instituted in certain areas during the war under the Maternity and Child Welfare Authority, by which selected women took in the children of mothers at work. "Sitters-in" might voluntarily or for a small payment keep an eye on the children when they are asleep, so that the mother and father might go out together; these might be either

older schoolgirls in need of a quiet place for their preparation, members of voluntary organisations such as
the W.V.S. or the Red Cross, or just friendly neighbours.

PSYCHOLOGICAL SERVICES

Child Guidance Clinics

The work of child guidance clinics in helping parents
whose children are maladjusted or who, perhaps on
account of their parental ignorance, are unable to
manage them, is of proved value, and these clinics
should be greatly increased in numbers.

Marriage Guidance Clinics

In the same way, marriage guidance centres—to help
men and women prepare for marriage, and to tackle
problems in their married life they are themselves unable to solve—though still somewhat experimental, are
proving themselves year by year of more use. The
Denning Report on the Divorce Laws (1947) has recom-
mended that they should become widespread and be
eligible for Government grants.

FAMILY RECREATION AND HOLIDAYS

At present little is done for the family on holiday.
Lodging houses and hotels are expensive and special
arrangements are rarely made by them for children.

"It is therefore suggested that the Government
should, through the agency of local authorities, semi-
public corporations (like the National Youth Hostels
Association, Camps Corporation, etc.), voluntary
bodies, and by appeals to private enterprise,
encourage and stimulate the provision of all these
necessary aids to family life. A diversity of family
holiday institutions should be provided from camps,

grouped cottage or bungalow resorts, to larger family hostels and holiday homes in the country and at the seaside. Crêches, play centres and nursing attendance should be available at all these places and reasonable charges made, with deductions in the case of large families. Specially equipped holiday trains might be considered. Drastic reductions in the cost of travel should be made (especially for holidays) by the method of cheap family tickets. These should be subsidised by the State if necessary." (*Fabian Report— "Population and the People."*)

Chapter 19

A NOTE ON MOTHERHOOD AND
OUTSIDE INTERESTS AND
OCCUPATIONS

How can we best tackle the problem of reconciling the need for more children with a mother's legitimate desire for interests, recreation and even occupation outside the home? We showed in an earlier chapter that the proportion of women who wish either to remain in their paid jobs after they are married, or to re-enter them after the child-bearing years are over, does not seem to be large. But there are certainly many—especially in the middle classes—whose feeling of frustration is great when their activities are entirely confined to home and children, so that they find neither time nor energy for interests outside. Unless some solution is found for their dilemma, the size of their families may well be even smaller than it is today.

In considering this whole problem, it is important to remember that we are seeking for policies to encourage a family *larger* than the one or two children who constitute the present standard pattern. I pointed out earlier that, if the birth-rate is to be raised to the average of nearly three children per family required for replacement, it may well necessitate a considerable proportion of married women having four children, and a smaller proportion—perhaps 15 per cent—having more than four. Whereas it may be possible even under present conditions for a mother to have one or two children and at the same time to carry on outside occupations and interests satisfactorily, would it not be extremely difficult for her to do so if she had a larger number of children?

FORMS OF HELP TO THE MOTHER

Everyone will agree on the desirability of a mother's having interests outside her home. The responsibilities of citizenship alone demand that she should know something about public affairs, and sometimes take an active part in them. As Gertrude Williams says: "Women, too, must learn that their responsibility to the home carries them far beyond its boundaries. The houses they live in, the food they can provide, the schools their children go to, the occupations for which they are trained, the wars in which they fight and maybe die, are all decided and shaped by forces which lie outside the individual home. The woman who accepts the home as her career cannot contract out of her communal responsibilities. The more seriously she recognises her duties to her family, the more readily must she accept full responsibility as a citizen." *

The claims of education and recreation must also be taken into account not only for the sake of the mother herself, but to help enrich her relations with her husband and children.

How can all these claims be recognised, and yet the mothers of today and tomorrow be asked, not only to have the present average number of children, but a definitely larger number? The answers to these questions can be found only in the whole complex of suggestions for a population policy which are put forward in this book and elsewhere—proposals, for instance, to enable the mother to have a few hours in the day free from children, to improve the design of houses, to provide modern domestic equipment and to give adequate domestic assistance. If carried out, these will help mothers to have much more leisure than is possible under present conditions. In addition, better nutrition,

* *Women and Work,* by Gertrude E. Williams.

better health and better training should enable them to tackle with greater energy and competence the domestic jobs which cannot be avoided.

Equally important, perhaps, is the change in the attitude of mothers to their work in the home which may result from a public opinion more sensitive than it is today to the importance of family life. Many mothers now enjoy making a success of their home, their family and their children. They realise the importance and interest of the work they are doing, and often feel that there is in it not more but less drudgery than in other occupations. It is those who are untrained and unskilled in regard to domestic affairs and the care of children, and previously unused to the work, from whom complaints are loudest. With the encouragement given by a greater measure of social approval and by improvements in practical conditions in the home, they may come to undertake their task with more zest and goodwill and less self-pity than is often the case today. Perhaps the fathers of tomorrow will also make a more important contribution to the care of their family than some of them do now, though many of them are already models in this respect. A member of the Women's Co-operative Guild, now middle-aged with four children, told me that she has never once scrubbed a floor, since her husband always regarded this as his job. He may indeed have been unique, but as education in family responsibilities grows and as a man's leisure time becomes greater, so may his sense of responsibility for wife and children express itself in a greater contribution to the mechanics of home-life.

MOTHERS IN PAID WORK

It is here that we are perhaps on more controversial ground. There are many who argue, as does Fru Alva

Myrdal, that it is wasteful both from the point of view of the individual woman worker and—what is even more important—of the productive capacity of the nation, for married women not to undertake any paid work. They point out that since the bearing even of four children takes only a limited number of years, this ought not to exempt a mother from paid work outside the home during the whole of her married life. It is conceded that while children are under 2 years or even under 5 (unless and until there are sufficient nursery schools and nurseries) most mothers need to stay at home, so that their children may be adequately cared for; but that once this period is finished, the mother should return to the labour market.

How far this point of view will prevail, I do not know. As I showed before, the average woman with children does not appear today to want paid work outside her home and will as a rule only undertake it if there is great financial need. She usually pays scant attention to such abstract questions as national productivity, and regards the maintenance of her family as the husband's job, unless she happens to be a textile worker (where it is part of the tradition for married women to work) or is engaged in a particularly interesting professional job.

Whatever may be the position when only one or two children are concerned, it seems questionable, where there are four or five children, whether the average mother's task will *ever* be sufficiently lightened for her to run her home satisfactorily, and at the same time have an outside job, however much help she may get from her husband and older children. For instance, even if the midday meal is provided at school or factory, there are week-ends and holidays and all the other meals of the day. A few moments' reckoning will show that, taking holidays, Saturdays and Sundays into account, children are at school for only little more than half the year. There is also the care of children or other members of the family when they are ill or in quarantine. The Penelope's web of mending must continue to be done at home, even if some washing and making of clothes can be carried on outside. The cleaning of the house and shopping remains, and even if domestic assistance can be provided for some, it is unlikely that there will ever be enough women available for this work to go round. The chief change we can hope to see is that the domestic assistance there is available will, with the help of public provision, be concentrated on mothers with young children and on invalids and old people. The mother, moreover, will never be exempt from her civic responsibilities and she needs to remain fresh enough to be a real companion to her husband and children. Can all these responsibilities be reconciled with the insistent claims of a paid occupation?

Part-time Work

So long as the demand for workers continues to be high, many employers will be prepared to tempt even those married women who have children into the labour market by continuing some of the arrangements made during the war for part-time work —which arrangements could well be extended from industry to teaching, administration, commerce and many other occupations. Part-time work is indeed obviously more suited to be combined with family life than are the rigours of a full day's work, and—given the development of the many aids to motherhood suggested elsewhere—the problem of reconciling work and family may be solved for some by these means.

At the same time, it must be recognised that from the economic point of view of the individual family, part-time work is unlikely to be of much help, since taxation, payment for the care of children, additional wear and tear on clothes, boots or fares, and the expense of meals out have all to be taken into account. Part-time work is probably useful more as an outside interest to the mother and from the point of view of the productivity of the nation than from that of financial gain. It is not, therefore, likely to have much influence on the birth-rate.

Removal of the Marriage Ban

Fru Myrdal calls the whole problem of work of mothers in the labour market not so much the mother's right to paid work as "the working woman's right to have children." She feels strongly that for young women to continue their paid occupations after marriage renders it easier from the economic point of view for them to start a family earlier than they could otherwise do.

In the end the decision as to whether a mother takes paid work outside her home or not is a matter for her and her husband to decide. Provided she is able to make adequate arrangements for the care of her children it must depend on where both her gifts and her wishes lie—and this may not always be in the home. All bans, therefore, legal or customary, on the employment of married women should be removed in the interests of her dignity, her freedom and her status. It should not be possible for an employer to dismiss a woman solely on account of marriage or because she is expecting a child. Already the provisions of the new National Insurance Act will make it possible for an employed mother to take a certain number of weeks off both before and after childbirth without too great a financial sacrifice. Help given by the community through Social Insurance or otherwise should prevent a mother from being forced into the labour market in order to keep herself and her children.

But for most women, work in the home is likely to come first, and it is to be hoped that the forces of public opinion will work mainly in this direction. As Gertrude Williams points out:

"In a world dominated by cash-values, the important work of the wife and mother is under-estimated because it is done 'for love' without payment. We are only just beginning to appreciate the fact that the value of any work is generally disregarded unless it gets social recognition, whether in the form of money payment or prestige. But the way to express our sense of the most important work that women do in society is not to pay them to do less important work; it is to recognise the unique contribution that wives and mothers make to the community and to give them the opportunity to do it properly. The job that a mother does for her children is not one that can well be accomplished by proxy, but also it is not one that can be done successfully in these days without society's full co-operation. More than economic factors are involved in this, though well-equipped homes, child allowances, good food and assistance with the burdens of domestic work are essentials. But much more important than these material aids is a shift in social values—the recognition of the wife and mother as a full and responsible member of the community in virtue of her work as housewife and not because she does an industrial job for a wage. . . . In war-time no one disputes the complete partnership of woman in communal life, and there is unstinted appreciation of her contribution to war industry. But rearing babies through happy, healthy childhood to independent maturity is even more important than wiring aeroplanes and it is a very much more absorbing and exacting task." *

ECONOMIC POSITION OF THE WIFE

It is naturally often felt to be a real hardship that a woman who works hard in the home all day often has no money she can call her own. Even among the most happily married couples such a wife—as Eleanor Rathbone used to point out—has to go to her husband for money with which to buy his Christmas present. The present position is due to the fact that a husband, though liable for the maintenance of his wife according to the standard of living customary in his social class, is in no way bound to give her any money of her own. Of course, in many working-class households a husband gives all his money to his wife, receiving back a small sum as pocket money. But the law demands nothing of the kind, and many husbands only give a housekeeping allowance, sometimes very inadequate in proportion to their income—or no regular allowance at all. What is therefore desirable is a change in the law regarding the mutual financial responsibility of wives and husbands, perhaps on the lines of the Swedish law. This gives both husband and wife each the right to half of their joint income, whether provided by one or both of the partners.

* *Women and Work,* by Gertrude E. Williams.

Chapter 20

OTHER SOCIAL SERVICES TO HELP FAMILIES

(a) TOWN PLANNING AND HOUSING

Town Planning

No longer must the need of families with children be sacrificed either to landlords—whether public authorities or private individuals—or to outworn custom. Planning authorities, whether in town or country, must make their primary object the creation of an environment suitable to give children what they need. Fortunately, this has been widely recognised, and in most plans for large towns that have been published the reduction of density in the overcrowded central portions has been regarded as axiomatic, however difficult it may prove to carry out. The need is also appreciated for the proper location of residential and industrial areas respectively, for the prohibition of ribbon development (so that houses may be built on the small and not on the main motoring roads), for easy access to the real country, and for the adequate provision of playing grounds, parks and open spaces, bathing and paddling pools. As Lewis Mumford points out:

> ". . . parenthood itself must become a central interest and duty; and the family and the primary group of workfellows and neighbours must become a vital core in every wider association. The rural conditions of stability and continuity, the rural association with the facts of growth and reproduction, of life and death, must become an intimate part of the environment of the modern city. . . ."

One of the most attractive features of the County of London plan and the plans of other cities is the establishment of neighbourhood units. These are small enough to be contained within main roads and large enough to provide the right-sized populations to feed a junior school, a community centre, several nursery schools, nurseries, mothers' and babies' and other health centres.

Housing

As regards housing, what is required? The very first need is that there should be as soon as possible a supply of houses and dwellings sufficient for each family to have its own, with a certain number of vacant dwellings, so as to allow for the necessary amount of moving from place to place which industry or a change in the circumstances of the individual may demand.

Next, houses should vary in size. There should be an adequate proportion of houses built with four or more bedrooms and subsidies should be payable with regard to them. These would be for the future large families. But what is equally important is that existing houses with four or five bedrooms—of which there is actually a sufficient number for the present large families—should be used for these families and not, as is so often the case, by smaller families who, just because they are smaller, can afford the larger rents. It is highly desirable that local housing authorities should so arrange priority among tenants as to ensure so far as possible that the larger houses are occupied by the larger families. When in later years grown-up children leave home, this should be followed by the family's transference to a smaller house. Suggestions as to how large families could be helped to pay higher rents will be found under children's rent rebates on page 197.

A larger proportion also of single- and two-bedroom dwellings is required, since at present we are wasting our housing accommodation by using, for instance, three-bedroom houses for families who can easily manage with one- or two-. It is indeed unfortunate for the future that the three-bedroom house should still represent such a large proportion of all houses planned.

As regards overcrowding, once our present standard of not more than two per room (children under 10 counting only as half) is reached, this standard should allow for a proper separation of the sexes, and for at least a minimum of privacy. Bedrooms should mostly be large enough to be used as bed-sitting-rooms and be able to be heated, in order that every member of the household may have some place where he can be quiet. All practicable labour-saving devices should be introduced—especially in connection with heating and lighting, with cooking food, and with washing persons and clothes. There should be adequate provision for prams and bicycles. With regard to blocks of flats, these should either be limited to four or five storeys in height or should have lifts. Balçonies which allow the passage of light, and soundproof walls should be provided.

(b) HEALTH

The many gaps in the health services, especially for married women and children, which were referred to in earlier chapters, will be filled when the National Health Service Act has been implemented. It is fortunately, therefore, no longer necessary to suggest what policies with regard to health ought to be, but merely to remind readers of the many forms of health services which will be covered by the Act. I have already referred in some detail to those which are grouped under Maternity and Child Welfare. The others include:

"(*i*) *Hospital and Specialist Services*—that is, all forms of general and special hospital provision, including mental hospitals, together with sanatoria, maternity accommodation, treatment during convalescence, medical rehabilitation, and other institutional treatment. These cover in-patient and out-patient services. The advice and services of specialists of all kinds are also to be made available where necessary at health centres and in the patient's own home.

"(*ii*) *Health Centres and General Practitioner Services*—general personal health care by doctors and dentists whom the patient chooses. These personal practitioner services are to be available both from new publicly equipped health centres and also from the practitioners' own surgeries." *

These services, with a few exceptions, will be available to everyone in the country free of charge.

(*c*) EDUCATION

School Education

It wa· pointed out in Chapter 15 that even with the present free secondary education provided under the 1944 Education Act, there might well be an increased section of parents who, in order to get the kind of school they most want for their children, will be prepared to pay even the higher fees that will inevitably be charged by independent schools. The only way of preventing this happening and of ensuring real equality of educational opportunities will be for the State schools

* Official Summary of the National Health Service Bill.

to become so good that they will at least equal, if not excel, the best of the independent schools.

This will involve an implementation of the many reforms which have been promised in the 1944 Act and elsewhere—such as a drastic reduction in the size of classes, a staff selected from the best products of our universities and training colleges, a large proportion of pupils staying on over 16, a high standard of buildings and equipment, holiday camps, playing fields and—still more important—a comprehensive and imaginative curriculum and a happy, democratic way of life. All this will take many years, but should be achieved in the end.

The development of school social services is provided for under the new Act. School meals are to be given free to all, and milk is already free. It is anticipated that the parents of nearly all children will want them to have milk, and that about three-quarters of the parents will want their children to have school meals.

The school medical service is to be improved. There are to be more medical inspections, and the establishment of treatment for minor ailments is to be compulsory. For the first time, local authorities will be able to give clothes and boots to children who need them.

Higher Education

The biggest educational reform, however, which still remains to be formulated, let alone achieved, is to provide free all forms of higher education, students being selected according to their fitness for the education or training in question. This principle has already been adopted in the defence services and as regards the training of teachers. It should be extended to all forms of post-school training, including both free tuition and, in many cases, maintenance at universities or technical institutions whether residential or non-residential.

When the usual period at the university or technical college is over, further forms of training should also be provided free on a scale sufficient to supply the country's demand for particular professions and occupations, students being selected in this case also according to their ability and suitability for the work.

If and when the Education Act has been implemented in as complete and imaginative a way as possible, and if and when the expense of post-school forms of education and training no longer constitutes an economic bar to entry into most of the higher professions and occupations, we shall at long last have knocked down one of the most important barriers against the larger family. Real equality of educational opportunity from the nursery school onwards should reassure parents that, however many children they may have, an appropriate education and training—the best of its kind—will be available for each one.

Part

THE QUESTION OF QUALITY

Chapter 21

HEREDITY AND ENVIRONMENT

"Where the city of the healthiest fathers stands,
Where the city of the best-bodied mothers stands,
There the great city stands."

Walt Whitman.

"Families when a child is born
Want it to be intelligent.
I, through intelligence
Having wrecked my whole life,
Only hope the baby will prove
Ignorant and stupid.
Then he will crown a tranquil life
By becoming a Cabinet Minister."

Lines "On the Birth of His Son,"
by Su Tung-p'o (A.D. 1036–1101).

HARDLY second in importance to the question of the numbers of the population is the question of its quality. To increase our numbers at the cost of the quality of our people would indeed be a barren achievement, and no population policy would be acceptable if it tended to sacrifice quality to quantity.

It is essential, therefore, to know as much as possible of how the differing characteristics and capacities of human beings arise. Is it possible through human agency so to influence matters that it is from the better categories of human beings in any society that future generations are mainly recruited? Hence we must try first to discover which are the factors which make for good human beings under the varying conditions of our lives today, and secondly we must enquire which of these are susceptible to conscious direction.

From time immemorial it has been recognised that heredity is of vital importance, and it has been generally accepted that many physical traits, such as the colour of the eyes, hair and skin, can be attributed almost entirely to its influence. It has also always been recognised that the more complex factors in the make-up of human beings, such as intelligence and other desirable qualities, are also largely due to the endowment with which we are born. Up till the last two or three decades, in fact, the experts claimed that they were entirely due to the forces of heredity. Experiments on identical twins (i.e. twins who have been developed from the splitting of the same egg fertilised by only one sperm) who have been reared apart show the most astounding resemblances among them both as regards their physical characteristics and their mental qualities. There are several accounts of identical twins who reached similar examination results, or who—though living apart—developed the same diseases at the same time. New experiments continually add to the evidence in this respect. An amusing recent one, for example, showed that such twins go to sleep in the same position and manner.

THE INFLUENCE OF ENVIRONMENT

Today, however, far more stress than before is laid on the contribution of environment. Dr. Julian Huxley states, for instance, that "one and the same genetic outfit will give different effects in different environments; characters are not and cannot be inherited in the sense in which inheritance is used by the geneticists. What are inherited are genes, factors and genetic outfits. Any character whatsoever can only be a resultant between genes and environment. . . . Thus we can see that the old question whether nature or nurture would be more important is meaningless. . . . In general neither nature nor nurture can be more important, because they are both essential."

From this it follows that the more similar the environment of two people, the more are the differences observed in them due to heredity. The opposite is also true. The more similar are people's genetic constitutions, the more likely are any differences to be the product of environment. When, therefore, there have been considerable differences in environment between two groups—such as different social classes—it is probable that some of these, though by no means all, would disappear if the environments could be rendered similar. Such groups may indeed differ as regards their inherited make-up; but the variations observed where the environment is very different are likely to be in part at least due to this fact. It has often been noticed, for example, that the average height of the working classes is lower than that of the professional classes. Very few today would suggest that this was due to any hereditary character, since it is now realised that an insufficiency of the right kind and quality of diet may result in a retardation of growth, a lack of physical energy and less resistance to infectious diseases—all of which would affect the stature.

Interesting figures were published during the war which illustrate this, since they show the amazing growth in height and weight of a group of Glasgow schoolboys after they had received a daily addition of milk to their diet. Therefore—to quote Dr. Julian Huxley again—"it is no longer legitimate to attribute the observed differences in physique and intelligence between social classes mainly to genetic or inherited factors. Genetic differences may, of course, exist, but the strong probability is that most of the differences are dependent on differences in nutrition. Further, the defective nutrition of the poorer classes is in part due to ignorance, but in a large measure to mere poverty. Until we equalise nutrition, or at least nutritional opportunity, we have no scientific or other right to assert the constitutional inferiority of other classes because they are inferior in visible characters."

THE INFLUENCE OF HEREDITY

At the same time, those who stress too much the importance of heredity are not the only ones in error. "While the view that the observed differences in achievement and behaviour between class and class, nation and nation, are primarily genetic, is untrue and unscientific, the opposite view that opportunity is all and that we need only work to reform the social environment, is precisely as unscientific and untrue. It must not be forgotten, moreover, that the environment itself tends to have a selective influence. The learned professions, for example, can only be entered by those whose intelligence is considerably above the ordinary, and it is not surprising to find—as, in fact, we do—that the children of professional men have on the average a much higher intelligence quotient than the children of casual labourers whose work does not make much demand on their intelligence." * Again, if a group of unemployed men is compared with the employed in the same occupation, it will usually be found that the unemployed are definitely of a less good type physical, mental or moral—since, when employment is scarce, it is those with some marked failing who would be the last to be taken on and the first to be turned off.

* Dr. Julian Huxley, *The Eugenics Review.*

THE QUALITIES DESIRED IN HUMAN BEINGS

What are the qualities in this country today which determine whether men are going to rise or sink in the social scale? "There must be some selective action, since with the passage of time some failures will accumulate in the lower strata, while the upper strata will collect a higher percentage of successful types."* On what does success depend? Is it upon the best kind of biological and human qualities, such as intelligence or co-operativeness, or is it due to the less desirable traits, such as cupidity, self-interest and ruthlessness? Although some people with unpleasant qualities have undoubtedly, thanks to these very qualities, enriched themselves and become members of the higher social classes, still in many occupations, including most of the professions and many of the managerial posts in industry, intelligence, energy and general co-operativeness are even more necessary for success. The higher the standards of value in any community the more likely are the really best people to get to the top.

It is often said that where human beings are concerned we do not know which inherited qualities we wish to encourage. In cattle-breeding, for example, we know that we want our cows to be good producers of milk and of meat, and to resist certain diseases; our race-horses to be swift and our draught-horses to be strong. But *is* it so difficult in the case of men and women to determine what we want? Most of us would support Dr. Blacker when he suggests that the following are characteristics "as to the excellence of which nearly everyone will agree: (*a*) Sound physical and mental health and good physique, including freedom from inherited taints. (*b*) Intelligence. (*c*) Social

* Dr. Julian Huxley, *The Eugenics Review.*

usefulness, including the moral qualities which make for good citizenship. (*d*) An energetic and optimistic attitude to life. (*e*) Love of children." This last he considers to be of the utmost importance in order that our best stocks in the true sense of the word should reproduce or more than reproduce their own numbers.

It will be noticed that—apart from the freedom from inherited taints—the other qualities suggested are all affected both by heredity and by environment. It is not easy to measure the extent to which the more complex characteristics are due to one or the other of these, or even to measure some of them at all. The furthest progress has been made in the measurement of intelligence—for which psychological tests have been devised, though these are able to take little account of the character as a whole.

Nevertheless, it has been found that children of very high intelligence are generally above the average in physique and in many other ways—though this in its turn may be partly due to their largely coming from homes which are better than the average.

INTELLIGENCE TESTS AS AN INDICATION OF QUALITY

Professor Burt shows that the basis of intelligence testing is that every child passes through certain stages of mental development, and that when it attains these various stages it can perform certain simple tasks, such as to tell the time, the day of the week, etc. The normal average child will pass a twelve-year test at the age of 12, but the retarded child will not reach it until it is somewhat older; the bright child will do the 12-year-old test when it is only 9. A good intelligence test consists of many items, all of which are of a practical kind, and are largely independent of education. In any case, practically every child receives sufficient education of the right sort to answer the questions correctly and to perform the tasks successfully if they are linked to the appropriate stage of development. Such tests have themselves passed the test of time; gifted children discovered by Terman in California twenty years ago have, as adults, turned out to be as gifted as was suggested by the results of their tests, and there are many other such examples.

But if it is agreed that by intelligence testing something important is being measured, is this due more to inheritance than to environment? If, for instance, you have got two different people measured by tests—one of whom shows an intelligence quotient of 90, and the other 110—how far is the difference of twenty points due to genetic influences and how far is it due to environmental differences? Professor Godfrey Thomson thinks it might be 50 per cent of one and 50 per cent of the other. Other authorities, on the other hand, suggest that a higher proportion—perhaps 75 per cent—is due to heredity. These conclusions are based on the enquiries referred to before into the relative intelligence of separated identical twins who, while possessing the same inheritance, have lived under different conditions; and on enquiries into the relative intelligence of foster-children and the foster-parents' own children who have had completely different heredity but the same environment.

Too much reliance must not be placed on intelligence tests, whether of children or adults, since some have grave defects. It is almost impossible to devise tests which can entirely leave out of account differences in environment, since different environments bring out or frustrate various kinds of qualities and capacities. This cannot fail to be reflected in the answers to any test, however scientifically planned. But on the whole they are considered to be as reliable a guide as we can have for the present.

IS THE QUALITY OF OUR PEOPLE DETERIORATING?

It has already been shown that the birth-rate in this country varies with the different social classes. Since 1921 there have been no official figures, but it is thought that the difference has diminished steadily from that date, and that the birth-rate of the unskilled workers is now probably less than one-third higher than that of the professional and business classes. This comparatively high birth-rate among the unskilled worker class, as was shown in the case of miners, is not now found among its more responsible and intelligent members. It is probably due to the inclusion in this class for statistical purposes, first of the subnormal element in our population known as the "social problem group," and next of the dull and backward, very many of whom have large families of children. It is among these groups that we find an undue proportion of defectives—physical, mental and moral— and of those of subnormal intelligence not necessarily amounting to certifiable defect. Caradog Jones showed in an enquiry he conducted in Liverpool, in 1926, that the one-third of the heads of families who were not manual workers were contributing about 20 per cent of the children; that the 20 per cent who were skilled workers were only contributing 15 per cent; while the 20 per cent who were semi-skilled were contributing 22 per cent, and the 30 per cent who were unskilled were contributing no less than 44 per cent. Two-thirds of the coming generation in Liverpool, therefore, were being recruited from the poorest sections of Liverpool parents—the unskilled and semi-skilled, amongst whom intelligence was least likely to be high.

Professor Burt has stated recently that it is almost certain that there is in this country a negative correlation between innate intelligence and the size of the family. The higher the number of children, the lower relatively does the standard of their intelligence tend to be—owing to the fact that it is usually the less intelligent families who have the greatest number of children. It would follow from this, he considers, that the average level of intelligence among the general population is declining at a rate of about two to four "mental months" per generation—which if continued would have serious cumulative effects.

An interesting table has been compiled by Professor Burt showing estimates of what would be the future distribution of intelligence among the different types of schoolchildren in the London area if the decline of two mental months per generation actually takes place:

Table 14.— The Future Distribution of Intelligence in
London Children

TYPE OF CHILDREN	I.Q.	1920	1950	2000
Scholarship	130	1·8	1·4	0·8
Secondary School	115–130	12·2	10·3	7·6
Good Average	110–115	35·1	33·4	29·9
Poor Average	85–100	37·5	38·6	40·5
Dull and Backward	70–85	11·9	14·2	17·9
Feeble-minded	70	1·5	2·1	3·3

It will be noted that as early as 1950 it is expected that nearly 55 per cent of the school population will be drawn from the poor average, dull or feeble-minded.

Several other psychologists agree with him. For instance, in an enquiry conducted by Fraser Roberts in Bath in 1939 among 540 children, in the brightest group he found a preponderance of children from small families. He found further that the social status of the father was directly related to the intelligence quotient of the children in the average and dullest groups, but not in the brightest groups. This meant that the bright children came from equally small families, whether their fathers were high or low in the social scale. Fraser Roberts concluded: "We cannot hope that the dying out of the very gifted who belong to the highest social categories will in part be made up for by an increase of the very gifted poor who are themselves just as infertile." Pearl Moshinsky, on the other hand, differs. In an enquiry she made in 1939 amongst 10,000 London schoolchildren, she came to the conclusion that a close relationship between the size of the family and intelligence applies only to the children of clerical workers and skilled labourers. There is thus a certain measure of doubt as to the universality of the relation between intelligent children and a small family. Fortunately the more depressing conclusions with regard to a decline of the level of intelligence in our people cannot be supported by any direct confirmation.

Moreover, with regard to other characteristics, such as moral qualities or freedom from nervous disorders, the differences between the social classes are much smaller.

THE FUTURE

How can we encourage the birth of children with better qualities and discourage the birth of those likely to have less desirable ones? William Penn's complaint of over 250 years ago that "Men are generally more careful of the breed of their horses and dogs than of their children" is still very largely true. There are, however, some definite steps we can take. We can, for instance, certainly discourage the breeding of children by certain subnormal categories of parents, such as those who are mentally defective or who have some form of hereditary mental or physical disease. In the case of mental defectives, the chances of two mentally defective persons having children who are either defective or diseased mentally or physically are very high. Even where there is only one parent mentally defective, such parents are rarely able to give the kind of home and family life children need. It is essential, therefore, that the recommendations of the (Brock) Report of the Departmental Committee on Sterilisation in 1934 should be carried out. These urge that there should be far greater provision than at present for institutions in which the mentally defective can be segregated and trained, and also that (under suitable safeguards) voluntary sterilisation of the unfit should be permitted. This operation, which is trivial in the case of a man and involves no danger in the case of a woman, enables those on whom it has been performed to have normal sexual intercourse and only prevents the passing of sperm in the case of a man and the production of ova by a woman. It is to be hoped that public opinion in this respect will soon have moved far enough to encourage this operation's being performed if the individual concerned, or his guardian on his behalf, so desires. This would enable those who have had it to lead as normal lives as their mental weakness permits without fear of passing on this weakness to possible children.

The same precautions should be taken with respect to those with a mental disease which takes the form of periodic attacks, in between which they are able to return to their homes and can and do produce children; also with respect to those who suffer from certain physical diseases which, even if not inheritable, prevent those suffering from them from being able to provide the right kind of home-life for children. Provision of this kind would certainly prevent the births of many individuals whose lives are bound to constitute a burden to themselves, and who have to make too big a demand on the social services of the country.

But a far more important question than prevention of births among a small section of the population, however undesirable, is the problem of how to encourage more births among those parents who possess the qualities making for a good and happy life. Here there is indeed no magic formula; but what is essential is to do everything that is possible to make it easier for people with these qualities to marry and have several children without too great a sacrifice on their part. Fortunately, the various policies we have already suggested, first to encourage the desire for children, and next to reduce the economic and material barriers and obstructions to parenthood, are most likely to meet with response from those who are vigorous, intelligent and responsible in themselves, and who have sufficient innate love of children to make it probable that they will want large families—provided the cost in energy, health and money is not too great.

The policies suggested in this book to improve the economic and social services should in themselves make for improvement in the quality of the population as well as for maintaining their numbers; but they are, perhaps fortunately, not likely to influence the selfish, the apathetic and the irresponsible.

Part VI

MIGRATION

Chapter 22

MIGRATION

"Some people," said Mrs. Gamp, "May be Rooshuns, and others may be Prooshuns; they are born so and will please themselves. Them which is of other nations think different."

Dickens, "Martin Chuzzlewit."

THE effect of migration on the numbers of our people has of recent years been small in relation to the effect of changes in the birth- or death-rates. But in the hundred years before 1931 emigration played a large part; and now, after the war, the Dominions at any rate are a lure to many of our young people. On the other hand, immigration in its turn may assume larger dimensions than ever before, either for political reasons, as with the present influx of Poles, or for industrial reasons, such as the urgent present need for more man-power, or because a decline in the population sets in and causes alarm.

EMIGRATION

Our policy with regard to emigration, therefore, needs to be carefully considered. In the hundred years ending in 1931, the United Kingdom lost something like 20 million persons, brought up and educated at its expense, who emigrated mainly to the United States and the British Dominions. But this constituted only a temporary relief from economic pressure, and from the beginning of the twentieth century emigration from the British Isles increased steadily, the peak being reached in 1913, when about 380,000 emigrants left for overseas. But after 1910 the stream flowed much more strongly towards the British Empire; indeed, not more than one-third of the aggregate number went to the United States; the conception of Empire unity was developing, and this gave an emotional pull to the Dominions. After the 1914–18 war, emigration started again and reached nearly 300,000 in 1920, but was reduced to under 200,000 when the 1921 U.S.A. restrictive quota came into operation. Emigration to Canada was also reduced about this time as a result of the Canadian policy of encouraging only agriculturists. In 1922 came the Empire Settlement Act, under which the British Government offered assistance to suitable persons in the United Kingdom who wished to settle in any part of the overseas Dominions. The total Government expenditure was limited to £3,000,000 and was not to exceed 50 per cent of the cost of any one scheme. The object was mainly to encourage land settlement, although in Canada domestic service also was included. No doubt many of those assisted would have emigrated in any case, and the Act could not prevent the total numbers from decreasing. This was not due only to its own limitations, however; many of the organisations which enthusiastically worked out schemes were inexperienced, and there were many failures and disappointments.

The Present Position

Up till 1931 emigration was a considerable factor. Since the last quarter of the nineteenth century down to that date there was a net loss of rather over 1 per thousand of the population on the average year, drawn largely from the most enterprising of our young people. After 1931, however, when the world depression began, the conditions in the countries to which most of our emigrants had gone—that is to say, the British Dominions and the United States—were, as regards unemployment, as bad as or worse than in Great Britain. The movement was therefore reversed and there were more returning to this country than leaving it.

A new source of immigrants opened in 1933, when Hitler came to power in Germany and the refugee movement thence started and continued up to the time of the war. The numbers involved were, however, far fewer than is usually thought, only about 90,000 having entered on this account. During the war, of course, all migration stopped.

The following table shows how migration modified the natural increase of births over deaths of the population:

Table 15.— Natural Increase in Population and Migration in England and Wales

	1861	1871–1881	1881–1891	1891–1901	1901–1911	1911–1921	1921–1931	1931–1939	1939
				(Per cent per annum)					
Natural Increase	1·36	1·51	1·40	1·24	0·24	0·68	0·59	0·30	0·27
Actual Increase of Population	1·32	1·44	1·17	1·22	1·09	0·49	0·55	0·44	0·60
Balance of Migration	0·04	0·07	0·23	0·02	0·15	0·19	0·04	0·14	0·33

It will be seen that nearly half the slight increase in the population between 1931 and 1938 was due to net immigration, whereas between 1911 and 1921 the natural increase would have been greater by one-quarter if it had not been depleted by emigration.

The Future

But what is likely to happen now? Already the Dominion Governments have indicated that they are most anxious for more immigrants. They realise that pre-war trends of their own birth-rates were heading for a decline in due course of their white population. Therefore they are rating very highly their capacity to absorb new elements from this country. In Canada, for instance, responsible statesmen are speaking of raising the population eventually from the present 11·5 millions to 60 millions or even considerably more. Australia has aspirations to raise her population from 7 to 20 millions, and New Zealand is also anxious for large additional numbers. They all wish to draw as far as possible from this country.

Unfortunately the class of emigrants the Dominions demand is mainly young adults under the age of 30. These are the more adaptable and are at the height of their physical powers, and the expenses of their up-bringing have been borne by the Mother Country. Between the two wars one-third of all the male emigrants from Britain were between 20 and 30, although this age-group only accounted for about 17 per cent of the total British male population. There is also a demand—especially from Australia—for children (war orphans and others) to be educated there.

In spite of the difficulties for ourselves if we encourage the emigration of our young skilled workers, the Government is prepared to fall in with the wishes of the Dominions out of friendliness, and in order to help them develop their industries. In March 1946, in response to a demand from Australia, it was announced that the Government offered to pay the passages of those who had fought in the war, and to assist those of others. This offer was extended in April 1947, the cost being shared between the Dominions and this country.

In principle it is highly desirable from every point of view—economic, social, technical and political—that there should be a free movement of peoples, and it is essential, therefore, that the individual citizen should be free to emigrate if he chooses and that the Mother Country should be prepared to help the Dominions. On the other hand we cannot afford to spare large numbers of our young people, since it is these we most need to keep. It must be a matter of give and take. The problem of our homeless children—towards the care of whom emigration can at best only make a very small contribution—can and should be solved along other lines.

IMMIGRATION

Throughout our history we have rarely encouraged any immigration on a big scale, except in a few well-known cases for the purposes of establishing or developing a new industry. We were, however, until 1933, traditionally regarded as an ever-open door for political and religious refugees, and it has been often from groups of this kind that many new industries from the Flemish weavers onwards have sprung.

Unfortunately the beginning of the Nazi terror coincided with a high rate of unemployment in this country, and public opinion for the most part not unnaturally resented immigrants of any kind. Those who came were accepted, therefore, for humanitarian reasons alone. The fact that many of them would contribute notably to the war effort, to scientific invention (including the atom bomb), industry and the arts, was not at that time foreseen. They started many new industries and employed many British workers. The condition of Europe today is such that a large number of individuals from some of the poverty-stricken countries may well wish to take up their abode here. What ought we to do about it?

No immigration policy can hope to be successful in this country unless full employment has come to stay and an adequate number of houses has been provided. Where there is competition, either for jobs or for accommodation or for both, immigrants from other countries are strongly resented. If, however, we succeed in solving both these problems within the next few years, then no great difficulty towards absorbing a considerable number of Europeans would probably be encountered. Already, owing to the shortage of man- and woman-power, members of the Polish Forces living here, and displaced persons, are being allowed to work in the mines, in industry and on the land. Girls from different European countries are being allowed to work as nurses and domestic servants. Apart from the Poles, this kind of immigration is so far on a small scale, but it may be increased later. But if immigration from these sources is to be a success, far more attention must be paid in the future than in the past both to encourage the kind of immigrants we need and to provide for their proper care when they arrive. In the past they have usually arrived without friends or knowledge of our ways. Those who came about the beginning of the nineteenth century from countries such as Poland or Italy were accustomed to lower standards of living and became an easy prey to the unscrupulous employer and others ready to exploit the helpless. Nevertheless, in the next generation a surprisingly large number made good and were easily assimilated.

In order to ensure that those who come will make desirable citizens, therefore, great care must be taken in the future to see that only those are admitted who are physically and mentally sound and free from any criminal record. The most desirable type will be young people—especially young married people—who come from countries the background of which will make it comparatively easy for them to be assimilated. These, whether potential or actual parents, will have received their nurture and education at no expense to this country, and are of an age at which they are able to work and to contribute their quota to the next generation.

In the case of children, many of them perhaps orphans of the storm, their upbringing can be looked upon as an investment which will bring its own rich reward, since they are obviously more easily assimilated than other age-groups. It is gratifying, for instance, to note what a large proportion of the children who came over in 1938 as refugees from Germany now feel themselves to be completely British, and fought and worked during the war as if they had been British born.

Undoubtedly, the types of immigrant who could be most easily assimilated would be those from the countries of Northern Europe. But the population trends in these countries are much the same as here,* so that their birth-rates before the war were either already too low for replacement purposes or so little above this level that if these pre-war trends set in again they will soon fall below. These countries, therefore, like ourselves, will not be anxious for any of the cream of their people to desert them.

With regard to Central Europe, there is very little chance of German nationals being regarded as desirable settlers for many years to come. The bulk of any possible independent immigrants from Europe are therefore most likely to be drawn from Italy and the Eastern European States where—before the war—the combination of a high birth- and a rapidly declining death-rate was leading to a large increase in the population. Many of the 100,000 Poles from the Allied Polish Army whom the Government is not prepared to force back to Poland

* See Chapter 24.

are likely to settle here. In the case of the U.S.S.R., with its wide-open spaces and spirit of aloofness, it is not likely that any of its inhabitants will either wish to or be allowed by their own Government to come to this country.

More difficult problems will be aroused by the possibility of immigration from the overcrowded Asiatic countries, such as India or China. Even though their nationals may not actually be excluded—particularly Indians, who are fellow-citizens of the Empire—still, it is unlikely that they will be positively encouraged, at least so long as there are strains nearer home from which to draw.

What would happen in future generations if, in spite of all that we can do to maintain our own population, it steadily declines, it is impossible to say. Immigration on a vast scale is indeed a counsel of despair, as it is a sign that we have failed to maintain the vitality and spirit to keep our own community alive. In the near future the obvious policy is to encourage foreigners to remain who are actually here or who can be attracted from countries most like our own, so that they can easily get to understand something of the British way of life. Nor should citizenship be long withheld after arrival. The process of naturalisation should be much simpler than at present, and immigrants should be expected and encouraged to acquire British nationality. They should be helped to get to know quickly our language and our traditions.

Part VII

POPULATION TRENDS OUTSIDE BRITAIN

Chapter 23 *

POPULATION TRENDS IN THE BRITISH COMMONWEALTH

(1) AUSTRALIA AND NEW ZEALAND

IN both these countries white settlers have sprung almost exclusively from the United Kingdom, and nowhere else does the Briton feel so much at home. White settlement in Australia dates from 1778, and the population, which is almost entirely white, grew very slowly until about 1900, when it was about 3·7 millions. It has nearly doubled itself since that time, and is now over 7 millions. The birth-rate, which in 1860–64 was at the astonishing height of 42·5, declined, partly owing to the slackening of immigration of young married people and partly to the change-over, as in this country, to the small, planned-family system. In 1903 the rate was 25·5, and the number of births per thousand women was decreasing steadily. Already in 1903 a Royal Commission, enquiring into the causes of the decline of the birth-rate, attributed the decline in the first instance to contraception and the growing use of abortion, but gave the reasons for these not as economic, but as unwillingness to submit to the strain, worry, physical discomfort and interference with pleasures, luxuries and comfort involved in child-bearing and child-rearing.

* This chapter owes much to *The Menace of British Depopulation* and *Population—Today's Question,* both by Dr. McCleary.

After 1912 the Australian birth-rate continued to fall, and reached a record low figure in 1924 of 16·3, when the net reproduction rate was 0·9. As a result of the recovery from the economic depression, the birth-rate rose to 22·3 in 1945, and the net reproduction rate had already reached 1 in 1943.

In New Zealand, a similar state of affairs has occurred. The birth-rate fell from over 40 per thousand in 1875–9 to 27·5 in 1908, and to 16·2 by 1935, when the net reproduction rate was 0·9, i.e. below replacement rate. During the war this rose in 1942 to 1·2.

The rise in the birth-rate in both countries since 1939 has probably been due to the same kinds of reasons as in this country, that is, to the greater economic security and to the increase in marriages brought about by war conditions.

(2) CANADA

In Canada, although the first white settlers came from France, since 1763 immigration has been very largely from this country, and the total population has risen from 250,000 in 1800 to 11·3 millions in 1938. The net reproduction rate has always been above 1, and in 1938 was 1·9, but for 1940–42 only 1·2. The outstanding factor in Canadian population trends lies in the difference between the birth-rates of the sections of French and British origin. The French and the British sections now form 28 per cent and 52 per cent respectively of the total population. In the province of Quebec, where the French-Canadians formed 79 per cent of the population, the excess of births over deaths in 1935 was 13·9 per thousand. In British Columbia, which is peopled almost entirely by settlers of British origin, the birth-rate was 13·6 and the excess of births over deaths was 4·3 per thousand. It would appear, therefore, that apart from immigration, Canada will be increasingly populated by the French strains. André Siegfried, writing in 1937, accounts for this firstly by the attitude of the Roman Catholic Church, whose instructions are largely followed by the French-Canadians, and partly by the attitude of the latter towards life and work, which is unlike that of other parts of America. "It takes the form of a moral discipline of the family exerted under the direct influence of the Church . . . it believes in hard work, immense thrift and self-discipline, accepts the doctrine of a large family as a duty, and restricts ambition to a sensible proportion."

(3) SOUTH AFRICA

Here we find 2 million white settlers, and $7\frac{1}{2}$ million coloured people. Of the white settlers, 58 per cent are Dutch and 34 per cent British. The Dutch are not being recruited from their mother country, while British immigration, although not large, was pretty steady till a few years before the war. Although the net reproduction rate in 1938 was 1·3 among the whites, this high rate was mainly due to the Dutch element. The British, who live chiefly in towns, followed largely the Australian and New Zealand example where the birth-rate was concerned.

In the Dominions in general it seemed likely, before the war, that the same road was being trodden as in this country, and that, although their net reproduction rate was higher than here, they were heading in the same direction, even if they were not yet quite so far on the way. The stage seemed set for a declining population in a few years' time. And yet look at their circumstances! Here are territories abundantly well fitted for people coming from the countries of North-West Europe. They are admittedly under-populated, and are anxious for very much larger numbers.

The standard of life is already so high that many of the economic handicaps—such as bad housing—which are imposed on parenthood in this country are not reproduced there. It is indeed difficult to account for the failure of these young and otherwise vigorous countries to produce the population they need both for defence and industrial expansion.

It may well be that as regards Australia and New Zealand, at any rate, the threat of Japanese invasion during the war has brought home the danger of a population too small for defence services. It has also produced an economic situation in which the potentialities both of Australia and Canada for industrial as well as for agricultural development are more than ever needed by a world hungry for manufactured goods as well as for food. It may be, therefore, that the wartime high net reproduction rate may remain and that their period of population expansion may be prolonged. Only time will show, but my own belief is that they are more likely to resume their pre-war characteristics in this respect and to be forced to invite immigrants from all parts of Europe, and even from Asia.

(4) INDIA

The rapidly growing population of India is about 400 millions, and constitutes nearly one-sixth of the population of the whole world. Its birth-rate is not quite so high as that of the U.S.S.R. and of many other East European nations, probably on account of its high maternal death-rate, which is 20 per thousand (as compared with under 2 per thousand in this country) and means that about 8 million mothers, many of them very young, die every year. The death-rate has declined from 34 per thousand between 1911 and 1920 to 21·8 in 1941. It rose, however, to 23·4 in 1943. The average expectation of life for men, which today in England and Wales is about 61 years, is only 27 in India. The standard of living is still appallingly low and under-nutrition is widespread. The all-over infant death-rate was 163 in 1941. Three-quarters of the population in the cities live in one-roomed tenements, often with no windows and frequently with more than one family to a room.

But in spite of these high death-rates and a low standard, the growth of the population is staggering. The most stubborn problems in India are not political, though it is the political situation on which the lime-light is mostly thrown; they are economic, owing to the rapid growth of population, with which the agricultural resources of the country cannot keep pace. Between 1921 and 1941, for instance, there was an increase of 27 per cent in the population, but a decrease of 2 per cent in the yield of cereals. Every improvement in social conditions, as has been pointed out in reports on India during the last fifteen years, is likely to be followed by a fall in the death-rate. As birth-control is practised only by a tiny minority, since it is opposed by the great bulk of the people on religious grounds, improvement in social conditions arising from greater productivity in industry and agriculture is nullified by a growth in the number of people—a truly Malthusian situation. The only hope is that as education increases, the regulating rôle of birth-control may be understood and accepted.

Chapter 24

THE INTERNATIONAL SITUATION

IT is not only in this country that population trends are of such vital importance. There is indeed no more important issue in any country, and in this chapter I shall try to give a brief account of the kinds of problems that arise elsewhere. It is, of course, impossible to deal with more than a few countries, even in the barest outline; but it will be possible at least to draw attention to the different types of problems in different countries and to group the latter to some extent according to their type.

So few statistics have been recorded since the war that I must deal mostly with pre-war conditions. In 1940 the total population of the world was 2,170 millions, of which the whites were little more than one-third. Dr. Kuczynski estimated that before the war, although certain countries with white populations, such as the U.S.S.R. and others in Eastern Europe, had rapidly increasing populations, the whites as a whole were no longer reproducing themselves.

BEFORE THE WAR
NORTH-WESTERN EUROPE

The tendencies in Europe vary according to whether we consider the countries in the north and west or those in the east and south. The table on page 253 shows the net reproduction rates of the chief European countries before the war.

A glance will show that at that time most of the countries of North-western Europe had already reached a stage at which they were not reproducing themselves,

Table 16.— Net Reproduction Rates in Europe before the War

	YEAR	NET REPRODUCTION RATE
Austria	1935	0·64
Belgium	1936	0·83
Bulgaria	1933–6	1·19
Czechoslovakia	1929–32	0·94
Denmark	1939	0·92
England and Wales	1939	0·81
France	1937	0·87
Germany	1938	0·94
Hungary	1938	1·00
Ireland	1935–7	1·16
Italy	1935–7	1·13
Netherlands	1937	1·12
Poland	1934	1·10
Sweden	1937	0·76
Switzerland	1938	0·79
U.S.S.R.	1937	1·70

or were likely shortly to reach that stage. This situation has been described as follows:

"By the early thirties fertility had declined so far that in most of the nations of North-western Europe it was no longer adequate for the maintenance of a stationary population. True, almost everywhere there were more births than deaths. However, this continued natural increase was misleading as to the likelihood of future growth. In many countries the excessive births existed only because the past course of growth had left large populations concentrated in the reproductive ages and relatively small ones in the older ages of high mortality . . . only the passage of time is required for such a situation to develop into one unfavourable to growth. The experience of France is a case in point. In the late thirties she had more deaths than births, and on the surface her position appeared unique. It was so only in that she led the trend. Her parental stocks in the thirties had been depleted by the low fertility of the years back to 1890. In England during the thirties fertility was lower than in France, but births exceeded deaths because the decline in the birth-rate had come at a later date, so that she still had a relatively large population in the child-bearing ages." (*"The Future Population of Europe and the Soviet Union," published by the League of Nations,* 1944.)

A similar situation was also found in the U.S.A., where the net reproduction rate between 1935 and 1940 was 0·97.

These countries had passed the period when the size of their population was mainly determined by their death-rate, and, whether their population declined or grew, it was regulated, therefore, mainly by the birth-rate which was for the most part determined by the number of children parents wished to have.

EASTERN EUROPE

If we turn to Eastern Europe, however, we find a different situation, in that the population trends were very much the same as they were in North-west Europe about seventy years ago. Thus the birth-rates were still high, but the practice of birth-control was beginning and had taken sufficient hold to lead in some countries to a sensible decline of the birth-rate. The death-rates, on the other hand, were declining rapidly, and accounted for the rapid increases in the population.

Many of the other countries in this group, however, such as Poland and Bulgaria, were already before the war faced with an extremely difficult situation. A rapid decline in their death-rate which had followed the spread of Western culture and scientific knowledge found them faced with the difficulty of providing even a most modest standard of living for their quickly increasing numbers. The need for ever more intensive cultivation and the continued division of land holdings had not yielded correspondingly greater production. Emigration played an important rôle only in Poland, and the chief solution before the war was found in a steady increase in industrialisation and drift to the towns.

The U.S.S.R., for instance, had before the war a net reproduction rate of 1·7 and was growing at a rate of 30 per cent per generation. It is expected that she will reach the gigantic total of 300 millions between 1970 and the end of the century. Owing to her immense natural resources, the rapid development of her industry and the rationalisation of her agriculture, she is at much the same stage from the population point of view as we were during the Victorian era in this country. In her case also, a rising standard of living will in all probability, in two or three generations' time, if not earlier, bring about a slowing down of her rate of growth.

THE WHITE PEOPLES SINCE THE WAR

Table 17.— Latest Net Reproduction Rates

COUNTRY	YEAR	RATE
Belgium	1941	0·672
Denmark	1943	1·140
England and Wales	1944	0·990
Netherlands	1943	1·305
Switzerland	1943	1·054
United States	1942	1·274

Since the war the picture has been somewhat different. In the North-western countries the birth-rate has risen considerably, as in this country, and probably for the same reasons, i.e. a greater economic prosperity, full employment and the emotional tension due to actual or anticipated war-time separations.

Except in those countries (such as Germany) where the war has caused devastation and led in its later years to a great fall in the birth-rate, it is probable that, as in this country, the present high birth-rates will remain for another two or three years covering the period of demobilisation and rebuilding. But the later trends I have indicated as probable in this country—a still lower birth-rate (due to better contraceptive technique and to a small marriageable stock) and a higher death-rate (due to an increasing proportion of old people in the population) are likely to lead in most of the countries concerned to an intensification of, rather than a departure from, pre-war trends. With regard to the other group of countries, in East and South-east Europe, it is extremely difficult in many places to know what the present situation is, owing to the effects of territorial changes, of war casualties and deaths due to malnutrition, and of migrations of people—forced or otherwise. Once the immediate effect of these has passed, in a few years' time, death-rates should continue to fall rapidly (as they were doing before the war) as medical knowledge and knowledge about nutrition increase—provided that economic conditions are such that, thanks to developments in industry and agriculture, higher standards of living become possible.

But as in the West it was the social changes following on the growth of cities and greater industrialisation which gave the impetus to a lower birth-rate, so is it probable that, as standards of living improve, and urbanisation grows, the birth-rate in South and South-east Europe will decline.

THE ASIATIC AND AFRICAN PEOPLES

If we now turn to the coloured peoples of the world, we find a different situation, though our information as to what is actually happening is very scanty. India, with 400 millions, and China, with probably over 300 millions, account between them for over one-third of the population of the world. In these countries, as also among the inhabitants of the other Asiatic countries and the native races in Africa, birth-rates are usually high, though kept down to some extent, not by birth-control, but by custom and a very high maternal death-rate. Death-rates, though declining also to a certain extent where modern scientific knowledge and health services have started, are still very high compared with our standards, so that it is the death-rates which mainly determine whether and how much the population grows.

Table 18.— Countries Arranged According to Zones

ZONE A	ZONE B	ZONE C
Western and Northern Europe	U.S.S.R.	India
North America	Southern and Eastern Europe	China
Australia	South and Central America	Other Asiatic Countries
New Zealand	Japan	Africa (Natives)

Mr. Titmuss divides the countries of the world into three zones: Zone A, where the main controlling factor is the voluntary birth-rate, since their death-rate is too low to allow a much further reduction; Zone C, which covers that part of the world where the main population regulator is still premature death; and Zone B, which includes those countries which are passing from Zone C to Zone A, i.e. mortality is being reduced while the birth-rate is still high, though some knowledge of birth-control is beginning to spread.

EFFECTS OF WORLD WAR II

In view of the very heavy losses both among the Forces and among civilians it is necessary—if at all possible—to make some estimate of what these amount to. With regard to the deaths in the Forces, this is not so difficult—although it is probably only in Great Britain that official figures have been published. It has been estimated that the total losses of all the nations involved in the war are of the order of $9\frac{1}{2}$ to 10 millions, or even higher.

The Axis losses have been estimated at rather over 5 millions, and were lower than those of the Allies, whose losses have been estimated at round about $6\frac{1}{2}$ millions. Of the losses of the Allies, far and away the heaviest were those of the Russians, which have been estimated at 5 millions, four-fifths of the whole Allied losses. The next highest were those borne by the British Empire, which lost in all about 375,000—of whom nearly 300,000 were from the United Kingdom. The U.S.A. was estimated as having lost 325,000. Of the Axis nations, Germany lost over $3\frac{1}{4}$ millions and Japan $1\frac{1}{2}$ millions.

The civilian losses are virtually incalculable, but must be immense. Not only has there been the transfer of millions from those countries—such as Germany and Poland—whose territory has been annexed by the U.S.S.R., but there was also the mass murder by Hitler of 3 million Jews, and the immense number of losses of those done to death in concentration camps, or who died as a result of the conditions under which both invasion and forced labour were carried on. And the end of the story is unhappily not yet. We cannot know how many have died or will die of malnutrition; or how many, though they escape death now, will carry into later life a burden of under-development and disease which will affect the death-rates for generations to come. Nor—in spite of the higher birth-rates at the beginning of the war in many countries—can we estimate the loss due to a birth-rate lower than it would otherwise have been owing to the death and absence of so many potential fathers. This may well be the heaviest of all the war losses as regards population. The Report of the League of Nations on *The Future Population of Europe and the Soviet Union, 1944,** sums up the situation as follows:

"The wounds of the first World War struck a resilient and rapidly growing population; through high natural increase this population could quickly close over its losses. The present struggle strikes at populations already growing much more slowly than a generation ago, and on the basis of past trends destined to decline. The wounds of the present war will, in a sense, never be healed. In some countries of Western and Northern Europe the total population may never again reach its pre-war size. Even in Eastern and Southern Europe war losses comparable to those of World War I will be made up much less rapidly than before, unless there is a marked change in fertility trends. Only in Soviet Russia are vital trends such that the tremendous losses can be absorbed without a serious check on population development."

* The Report, published in 1947 by the League of Nations, estimates civilian deaths in the U.S.S.R. as 9 millions, and the "deficit" in the birth-rate as accounting for 6 million unborn children.

Chapter 25

POPULATION POLICIES IN OTHER COUNTRIES

In view of the fact that during the thirties so many of the countries of North-west Europe—including France, Germany, Scandinavia, Holland and Belgium—had a birth-rate too low to admit of replacement, and that others—such as Italy—were travelling rapidly in the same direction, it is not surprising that the alarm had been sounded, and that the Governments of these countries were making attempts—some more and some less thoroughgoing—to tackle the problem.

It will be remembered that there are three ways in which the population of any country can be increased: (1) through an increase of immigration; (2) through a reduction of the death-rate; and (3) through an increase in the birth-rate. Of these three, the increase in the birth-rate is far and away the most important, but a brief reference must first be made to the other two.

Immigration "provides human capital free and at once" as a substitute for the more costly process of rearing and educating one's own children; but it is not easy for any country to absorb comparatively large groups with alien speech, religion and culture. Although, therefore, "nations seeking to avert population decline may be willing to accept immigrants, they can be expected to be circumspect of them," * and it is unlikely that immigration from Eastern and Southern to Western Europe will ever be on a big scale. From the beginning of the century, however, France has been in the habit of welcoming workers from Spain and Italy and, before the war, from Belgium, Poland and Russia.

* *The Future Population of Europe and the Soviet Union.*

REDUCTION OF THE DEATH-RATE

In nearly all the countries in North-west Europe the spread of social services and the increase in medical knowledge had, before the war, led to a fall in the death-rate so great that there was not very much farther to go in this direction, except in the case of certain sections of the population who were still living under bad conditions—especially with regard to infants under 1 year. In most of these countries with a low birth-rate the population would still have failed to replace itself at pre-war birth-rates even if all deaths under the age of 50 had been eliminated.

POLICIES TO INCREASE THE BIRTH-RATE

The main problem, therefore, for the countries concerned was how to raise the birth-rate. The policies adopted fall into the two familiar categories: (1) that of propaganda and education, and (2) that of financial assistance to parents and of the development of the social services for mothers and children. This being so, it is inevitable that many similarities in methods should be observed among them. But underlying these similarities there were also marked differences of principle between countries with authoritarian régimes and those in which democratic ideals were aimed at.

In democratic countries, such as Scandinavia, stress was laid on the freedom, happiness and well-being of the individual, both parent and child. It was recognised that a child must be welcomed by his family, and that the policies put forward should contain no repressive element, whether in the guise of preventing women from taking paid work, of prohibiting information on methods of birth-control or of imposing financial hardships on bachelors and the childless. The appeal for more numbers was made on the grounds of keeping the community stable in numbers and age distribution in order to prevent its slipping away altogether.

In the totalitarian countries, such as Germany and Italy, on the other hand, to have bigger families was represented as a duty to the State, whether the children were wanted by parents or not. Information on methods of birth-control was either banned or frowned upon and the sale of birth-control appliances forbidden. Married women were apt to be prevented from entering the labour market, and taxes were imposed on bachelors. This propaganda was almost entirely based on the need for more men for military and aggressive purposes.

We must, however, beware of condemning any given policy because it is put forward by a country from whose general political attitude we differ; since the policy in question may not necessarily be objectionable in itself, but made so by the motives behind it and the arguments put forward in its support.

There is little space here to give anything but a very brief account of policies in the different types of countries which have so far paid most attention to population problems. *France* was the first country in modern times to adopt deliberate policies to increase the birth-rate. About seventy years ago voluntary associations gave a wide publicity to the situation, and their propaganda efforts were strongly reinforced by Émile Zola in his famous novel, *Fecondité*. A determined attack was carried out on infant mortality, and the first infant welfare centre held anywhere was established in Paris in 1892 and resulted in a steady fall in the infant death-rate. Believing that the causes for the decline in the population were mostly economic, France was the first country to adopt a family allowance system, family allowances being given by a few individual employers as early as 1854, not so much to increase the birth-rate as for purposes of child welfare. Family allowances spread rapidly during the first world war and were finally made compulsory in the more important occupations in 1932. The French scheme is an industrial one, the money being provided by employers who pay into industrial pools, from which payment is made to the individual worker. Up till quite recently the allowances have been very small, though they increase with each child, and could and did have no perceptible effect on the birth-rate. Before this war, however, and again since, these payments have been raised considerably. In 1938 they were made compulsory for the whole range of industry and agriculture.

In 1946 both maternity grants and family allowances were increased to a very high level, allowances being paid so long as a child is at school. Allowances are now related to the average Departmental wage. For two children they constitute 20 per cent of the wage, for three 50 per cent, and for four 80 per cent, and so on. There is an additional allowance payable to families where there is only a single wage earner, under which 20 per cent of the wage is paid for the first dependent child (reduced to 10 per cent after it reaches the age of five), 40 per cent for two dependent children, and 50 per cent for three or more.

The history in *Belgium* is very similar. Family allowances were made compulsory for all firms in 1930, but the sums have been too small to provide any incentive to parenthood. They also have now been increased.

In *Italy* a great propaganda campaign and other policies aimed at increasing the birth-rate were inaugurated by Mussolini in 1937. The repressive tendencies were marked; birth-control propaganda and the sale of contraceptive appliances were forbidden and bachelors were not only taxed as such, but the best appointments in the Government service were given to family men. Family allowances were started and many measures were taken to encourage a return to rural life and to diminish the development of large towns. All the resources and pageantry of the State were summoned to bestow public approval on parents of large families. But in spite of all these efforts the birth-rate continued to fall.

Policies initiated in Hitler *Germany* are now only of historic interest, but I will include them here, since they made a considerable stir at the time. Propaganda was intense and was based mainly on militaristic and nationalistic ambitions. Women were exhorted to do little more than produce children, whether in marriage or outside it. Among other repressive measures, birth-control was prohibited, and until rearmament claimed women's labour, women were excluded from factories and from universities, etc. Birth-control was forbidden and the penalties against illegal abortion—which in 1933 was estimated to amount to anything from two-thirds of the live births to a number equal to them—was strengthened. It is claimed that illegal abortion was reduced to such an extent that this in itself would account for the rise in the birth-rate from 14·7 in 1933 to 20·3 in 1939. Bachelors were taxed and many privileges given to fathers of families. As regards financial inducements, there was first an extensive policy of marriage loans—25 per cent of each loan being cancelled for each child born within a certain period. Next, reductions were given for school fees, children's rebates were given on rent, school meals were given to poor children and holidays provided free. It is impossible to say—except for the apparently dramatic drop in abortions—what effect Hitler's policy had. Certainly parents who received the marriage loan did not seem to have bigger families than those who did not receive it.

It is not surprising that, in the latter stages of the war, there was a 25 per cent drop in the German birth-rate.

The *U.S.S.R.*, with its boundless resources and far-flung dominions, in 1944 developed a thoroughgoing population policy as part of its resolve to try to make good some of its appalling losses during the war.

First, it provides for a considerable increase in the allowances paid to mothers of large families, including a bonus at the birth of each child from the third, and monthly payments from the second to the fifth birthday for each child from the fourth. Although these allowances cease when a child is still so young, the payments are generous and increase with the place in family of the child. The bonus on the birth of the fourth child is 1,400 roubles, rising to 5,000 roubles for each child from the eleventh onwards. The monthly allowance on behalf of the fourth child is 80 roubles, rising to 300 for the eleventh and subsequent children. Payments of 120 roubles at the birth of each child are also made by the Social Insurance Fund, layettes being provided at this price. Unmarried mothers receive special allowances up to the third child until it reaches the age of 12; when they have more than three children they are entitled to the allowances for which the married mothers are eligible. They may send their children to institutions to be brought up at the expense of the State, but can have them back at any time if they wish.

Next, special privileges are provided for pregnant women and nursing mothers, and the general protection of mothers and children is increased. For instance, twelve weeks' leave of absence for women workers is allowed over a confinement, when special additional allowances are paid; overtime and night work is prohibited for nursing mothers, who, with pregnant women, receive supplementary food. There is a reduction in nursery or school fees for parents with three or more children and increased provision of children's clothing at special prices. In accordance with Soviet custom, great value is placed on public approbation, and a series of medals for mothers has been established, ranging from a "motherhood medal" for mothers of five or six children to the "heroine mother medal" for mothers of ten or more. In addition to all these inducements, financial and social, special taxes are imposed, with certain exceptions, on single men and women and on citizens with less than three children. Birth-control is frowned upon and abortion permitted only for certain specified reasons.

Let us now consider *Sweden*, since it is in the Swedish population policies that we find an approach to the population problem most like our own. It relies on education and practical help for parents and eschews repression of any kind. In the years before the war the net reproduction rate was 0·7, a little lower than our own (in Stockholm it was as low as 0·4), but in 1934 public opinion was aroused by a book called *The Crisis in the Population Problem*, by Professor and Fru Myrdal. It became a best-seller, and as a result of the intense interest aroused, a Royal Commission was appointed in 1935 to go into the whole question. This Commission sat till 1938, and has issued not only one but a series of reports. Many of its recommendations, mainly with regard to social services, have been carried into law. But the war has prevented development being as rapid as it otherwise might have been.

A second Commission was appointed in 1941 to work out policies more in detail.

The need for children to be wanted children is strongly emphasised, and so that children should not be born where they are not wanted, or where the quality of the parents is such that they should not exist, stress is laid on the importance of giving information on birth-control. As Myrdal says, "We do not want to keep up our birth-rate by causing the birth of unwanted children who have to thank ignorance or bad luck for their existence." For the same reason abortion may legally be performed if a child is not wanted. No disabilities are imposed on unmarried persons, and although a marriage-loan scheme was introduced to avoid dependence on hire-purchase, this was not given, as in Germany, in order to induce women to give up paid work, and was not repayable on the birth of children. Other repressive policies were also avoided. Women since 1937 have not been allowed to be dismissed on marriage, and the employment of married women is to be safeguarded during a three months' absence for child-bearing purposes.

Swedish policies aim at encouraging population growth through improving the general conditions of life, especially for the poorest members of the community. They pay particular attention to the promotion of public health, particularly of mothers and children. Swedish maternity and child-welfare services were in many respects not as advanced as our own, so that the list of recommendations has a familiar ring. They include the provision of home-helps, day nurseries, the appointment of guardians to watch over the interests of mothers with illegitimate children (14 per cent of all births are illegitimate, as compared with 6 per cent before the war in this country). They also include the provision of free maternity attendance at home or in hospitals and a great increase in infant welfare centres. Some of these recommendations have already been carried out, others are still to come. As regards financial assistance, although a general scheme of family allowances has not been adopted, a maternity benefit of 75 krone is paid to a mother where the parents have under 2,000 krone a year. Income-tax rebates are allowed on a scale very much the same as our own, but children's rent rebates have been established to a far greater extent and of a much higher amount. Where there are four children they amount to 40 per cent of the whole rent, and where there are eight children, to 70 per cent. The sitting Swedish Commissions appear, moreover, to have discovered a way in which rent rebates can be arranged for where houses are privately owned. As regards schoolchildren, a certain number of poorer children are provided with free meals, and there is a movement to give free secondary education.

So much for the practical proposals, which on the whole do not amount to more than is already provided here, and are not likely *in themselves* to achieve the ends at which they are aimed. But the fact that the Swedish birth-rate has gone up to 19·3 from 13·9 before the war is interpreted in Sweden as the result of the propaganda with regard to family life and to the happiness of having children. Larger families are becoming more fashionable, especially among better-off people, where the birth-rate is now higher than among the more cautious and less well off among the middle classes. If this interpretation is correct, it is a striking tribute to the change which can be effected mainly by influencing public opinion.

Chapter 26

GENERAL CONCLUSIONS

"There is no wealth but life."
Ruskin.

MY task is now completed, however inadequately it may have been performed. I have given the facts with regard to our population trends before and after the war and my views as to their causes, and have tried to make a reasonable guess as to the future. I have shown that before the war we were heading for a steady decline in the number of our men and women of reproductive age every generation, which would, if unchecked, lead to a literal fading out of our population. I have shown that the dramatic rise of the birth-rate during the war can be accounted for by a happy coincidence of causes, temporary in character, such as economic prosperity, an unusually high proportion of young people of marriageable age and an emotional tension, which together led to an unusual number of marriages. But I have shown also that the number of births following these marriages has not been correspondingly large, and that there has been probably only a slight increase in the crucial figure—the size of the average family.

Until the Royal Commission's Report is published there will be, it is true, many gaps in our knowledge as to what is happening; and at present *we* still have to guess where *they* will be in a position to know. But, in spite of these limitations, I have tried to answer the question whether the pre-war net reproduction rate of 0·8, based on the pre-war birth- and death-rates, is likely to return. I have shown that in my view it is unlikely that in the future, failing any unexpected influence, the birth-rate will be even as high as it was in 1939. The present birth-rate does not as yet reflect sufficiently accurately the small size of the family desired by many parents under present circumstances—since birth-control methods are today often either not made use of, or if used often fail. Improved contraceptive technique would probably, therefore, be followed by a considerable fall unless there were big compensatory influences to bring about a real increase in the number of children average parents wish to have. I have also shown that at the other end of the scale the increasing proportion of old people in our population must lead eventually (other things being equal) to a higher death-rate.

Everything, therefore, seems set for the population beginning to decline in a few years' time—though the temporary increase in the birth-rate will no doubt continue for a few more years as a result of the reunion of families after the war, and of the provision of adequate housing accommodation. The real cause for alarm is, not that some decades hence we shall almost certainly be a few millions less, but that if the same attitudes towards the size of family wanted continue, every generation will be smaller than the last, so that we shall be faced some time during the coming centuries either with a country nearly empty of people or (and this is perhaps more probable) with a people reinforced by immigration and consisting of a mixture of our present British stock with that of peoples mostly from Eastern Europe or Asia.

Next, I have suggested many reasons—personal, philosophic, psychological, political and economic—why it would be a world calamity if the British people both in these islands and in the white Dominions were either to become very much reduced in numbers or to die out

altogether. The chapter dealing with possible consequences of a declining population was perhaps the most
difficult to write and consisted inevitably far more of
opinions than of facts; and with regard to opinions it
is almost impossible to be objective. Still, I hope that
the great majority of those who happen to read this
book will agree, first, that more children tend to a richer
family life; and secondly, that Britain, at least as much
as any other great nation, has an immense part to play
in the world; that her standards of value—the democratic ideals of freedom, kindness, tolerance, justice and
the rule of law—are of such fundamental importance to
the welfare of the world that it is highly desirable that
her present considerable share of influence should at
least be maintained, if not increased. While it is true that
mere numbers of heads do not in themselves enhance
either influence or prestige—since this mainly depends
on intelligence, energy, tradition and values—still,
numbers are a limiting factor. To fall much below the
present level of population in this country would inevitably relegate us to the category of small nations and
seriously reduce our influence, political and cultural.
In countries like Sweden, Denmark, Holland or Belgium there is much to admire and a very high level
of civilisation has been reached. But their influence on
the world is negligible compared with that of Great
Britain, whose culture is in most respects as high or
higher and whose numbers are very much greater.
Small countries can now exist only if permitted to do so
by the larger ones.

The viewpoint changes somewhat if one considers the
future, not of Great Britain alone, but of the whole of
the British Commonwealth—since it is largely because
our own 47½ millions can combine with the Dominions
that we are still a great Power ourselves. Can one in

the future expect closer relationship between the Dominions and the Mother Country, or are they all likely to become more detached from one another? If one could envisage a closer relationship between them, it might well be considered desirable to have a lesser concentration in the British Isles—say 30 millions—and to try to build up a denser population in Canada and Australia. If that is so, emigration from this country to the Dominions would have to be planned from both ends on a much bigger scale than at present. But all this is extremely speculative, and in this book we are confining ourselves in the main to Britain's own problems.

I pointed out that a possible alternative to an ever-smaller population would be one replenished, not by people from North-west Europe, since these are likely to have the same problem of population decline as ourselves, but by those from South-eastern Europe and Asia—races with many virtues and qualities, but whose outlook and ideals are likely to be very different from ours today, and whom we should find it extremely difficult to assimilate. What is more likely actually to happen is that as our population shrinks this will only be partially compensated for by more immigration. For the smaller the population, the more, as time goes on, is any nation likely to resent the entry of large numbers of people very different from themselves.

A greatly reduced population is a fate that no people of spirit who love their country can contemplate with equanimity. It is not over-nationalistic fervour or imperialism in an unpleasant sense to wish one's own people to survive—it is a natural desire. The danger to our future existence must be resolutely faced; we must be more conscious in the future than we have been in the past of how perilous our situation may eventually become.

What can we do about it? As I have emphasised over and over again, the problem is in the main a psychological one—a question of values—though the practical handicaps to a larger family are real and must be mitigated. Let the individual citizen feel his responsibility for maintaining his community in peace as he does in war. This is a newer aspect of a citizen's duty than is defence in war, which has been recognised for so long that it is now taken for granted, whatever the sacrifices it may demand. Defence from disintegration from within is less romantic, more sustained in its demands, and the need for it much less easy to recognise. But only if the essential need for it is appreciated and acted on will the present small-family pattern change. The ordinary parent must come to realise that the number of children he has is not *only* his own affair, but the affair of the community as well. This is no question of the State's bullying people into parenthood. Fortunately, this is a sphere in which control is impossible! Parenthood must be wholly free, and to withhold access to knowledge of methods of family limitation is unthinkable for a free people. But those who love children and family life—and the numbers of these may be increased as skill in bringing up children becomes more general—should be helped and encouraged by public esteem, and by the provision of greater financial assistance and more social services on their children's behalf.

The necessary changes in attitude can only be brought about by public opinion, and in this book an attempt has been made to trace out the various ways— both direct and indirect—in which public opinion, both of potential parents and of the nation as a whole, may be influenced. To a considerable extent this is an educational question. Education both for citizenship and for family living must play a larger part than at present in our schools and colleges, our universities and adult classes, our welfare centres and women's organisations. The provision of official information on the facts of the situation by the Government, the Press, the B.B.C., and the cinema all have a large part to play in bringing about a state of affairs where a larger family than that of today is to be looked on as a matter for pride and joy instead of as a misfortune or a joke.

Once the wish for more children, whether for personal or other reasons, has been aroused among potential parents, the community must show its sense of the importance of children in the help that it is prepared to give them—help that must continually keep pace with higher standards of living. It must be regarded as a first call on the State's activities that it should recognise its duty to ensure its own survival and the good quality of its people, and that it should do all that lies in its power to provide an environment—physical and psychological—suitable for children. It must encourage the birth and bringing up of children among parents well fitted physically, mentally and emotionally to have them, but should discourage the production of families by the really unfit.

Of recent years many fine beginnings have already been made. Under the new Education Act, for instance, it is hoped that every child will have the education best suited to its individual ability and aptitude—though the free provision of higher education still remains to be achieved. The National Health Service Act will enable due attention to be paid to the health and physical needs of mothers and children, and provides for very necessary domestic help to mothers in their homes, and more nurseries and "sitters-in" to relieve them from being tied. Town planning and housing schemes are making the health, enjoyment and safety of children a prime consideration. The financial burden on parenthood is being lifted to some extent with the establishment of family allowances, free school meals, children's income tax rebates and children's rent rebates, maternity benefits and allowances. Although these are not on a big enough scale, they point the way, and in the end a real feeling of partnership between parents and State should be brought about. Above all, the State, by its handling of financial, industrial and economic matters, can do much to prevent shortages, want, and unemployment; and by wise political action in the international sphere can do its share, or more than its share, to contribute to co-operation among nations and the lifting of the fear of war.

I have suggested that the measures proposed should be taken promptly and generously, so that—once the problem of providing adequate housing and educational facilities has been solved—our aim should be to establish a stationary population with an average family of three children in about ten to fifteen—or at most thirty —years' time.

If the longer period of time is required, the population will probably have fallen by some millions before it is stabilised. Some of the unfortunate results of this might be mitigated if in the meantime, either through emigration from this country or through a higher birth-rate in the Dominions, the distribution of population within the British Commonwealth had altered in favour of the latter. Providing close links are forged between the Dominions and the Mother Country, our cultural traditions and political ideals would remain, even if the numbers in Great Britain fell. It will, however, be necessary for the Dominions themselves, especially for Australia, to adopt policies similar to those I have outlined. It is even more necessary in their case to aim at a rising population. Under-population with them is still so obvious that their situation calls for something more than mere stability. India, on the other hand, must aim at a decreasing birth-rate.

Does it then need both a great psychological and emotional change as well as an economic revolution to raise the birth-rate in this country to the extent necessary to maintain a stationary population in a generation? Or can these ends be achieved by a steady education of public opinion to stress the need for an average family of about three, together with the promotion of general economic security and the provision of other aids to parents, so that those who care for children will be able to combine a larger family with a high standard of life?

No one can say whether the change required amounts to a revolution, psychological, social and economic, or whether it is easily within the realm of possibility or even probability.

My own view is that no revolution is necessary, though a change certainly is—a change by no means impossible to bring about once the need for it is appreciated. In fact, as I have shown, there are some signs it is already taking shape. But it may not come by itself, and it is in the hope of making a small contribution to the work on its behalf that I have written this book.

Chapter 27

SUMMARY OF RECOMMENDATIONS

I. THE TARGET

(1) That we should aim at *a birth-rate which would secure a population at not much less than its present level* and which would remain stationary as regards numbers and stable as regards age composition.

(2) That the *transition period* should be as short as possible compatible with the need for providing the social and material conditions in which parents can be asked to have more children.

(3) That this should take from *ten to fifteen years* and should certainly be achieved in *thirty*.

(4) That the *average number of children* per family should be increased from round about two to round about three.

(5) That the *family size in this country should range from two to seven.*

II. PRINCIPLES OF POPULATION POLICIES

(6) That the Government should deliberately adopt *policies designed to influence population changes* in the above direction and should give *one Government department* the duty of considering what is necessary for this purpose. That this department should also have the responsibility for considering the probable effects on population issues of any action the Government may wish to undertake.

(7) That children should be *wanted children.*

(8) That a more courageous and robust *faith in life* should be encouraged among those who do not want more children owing to a defeatist attitude to life.

(9) That those parents who desire more children

should be encouraged by *the community's taking a generous share of the practical and financial sacrifices involved in parenthood.*

(10) That the Government's policies should aim at *improving quality, saving life and postponing premature death.*

III. EDUCATION IN RESPONSIBILITIES OF CITIZENSHIP AND FAMILY LIFE

(11) That the State should help to develop among all citizens a *sense of responsibility for the survival of the community and a greater appreciation of the value of family life.*

(12) That with this end in view, the Government should provide *information to the public* with regard to population trends; that the different Ministries concerned with family life should provide factual material; or, alternatively, that a special Government department or part of a department should collect information and conduct research on all aspects of the population problem. If, as suggested in (6), a special population department is set up, that department should undertake the collection of information and research.

(13) That the *co-operation of the Press, and B.B.C., of producers of films, of the theatre and of writers on public affairs* should be obtained for the dissemination of information and education on population issues.

(14) That *the education of parents in child-care* should be carried out both by officials in touch with the home —such as health visitors, certain teachers and school attendance officers, who should be properly equipped for this task; and by maternity and child welfare centres, marriage and child guidance clinics and many kinds of voluntary organisations.

(15) That schemes for formal adult education should include a far larger number of *classes and discussions*

on social studies, philosophy and ethics, physiology and psychology, hygiene, family relationships, child-management and the domestic crafts.

(16) That a larger part should be played by the schools in *training young people for their social responsibilities,* so that when they grow up each may "passionately desire to be a perfect citizen knowing how to rule and how to obey with justice."

(17) That for this purpose every effort should be made through religious and ethical training and through the way of life of the school to help boys and girls *appreciate high standards of value in public as in personal affairs.*

(18) *That children should be helped to know* what they can understand *about the communities in which they live.*

(19) That *education in family living,* including sex education, the technique of running a home and of bringing up children, and an appreciation of the fundamental values and happiness of family life should be given in schools by formal and informal methods suitable to the age of the child.

(20) That the balance of the *curriculum in girls' schools* should be modified so as to take into consideration the fact that marriage is the most likely career for the great majority of girls.

(21) That *co-education* should become more and more the rule.

(22) That the *staffs* of all schools for older children should include members of both sexes, married and single.

(23) That the importance of dealing with education for citizenship and for family living in *secondary schools* be realised, as only a few short hours per week will be available for all purposes for young people in county

colleges, though the county colleges should do what time permits in these respects.

(24) That for *young people in youth organisations* stress should be laid on *education for citizenship* through the way of life of the club, through knowledge of the modern world and training in clear thinking and ethics.

(25) That *education for family living* on the lines suggested for the schools should be given by youth organisations through talks, classes and films; that in particular engaged or newly married couples should have the opportunity of attending classes in family relations, homecraft and child-care.

(26) *That teacher training courses* should be reorientated so as to give all teachers in training sufficient knowledge of sociology, philosophy and biology to help them understand the social and family backgrounds of the children they will have to teach.

(27) That *refresher courses* in education for citizenship and family living should be arranged for the teachers now in schools.

(28) That *universities* should regard it as one of their prime functions to help their students gain a *philosophy of life and a standard of values,* and for that purpose should provide courses in philosophy and ethics, biology and psychology, economics and politics, as part of the general education for all students.

IV. PRACTICAL AND FINANCIAL ASSISTANCE TO PARENTS

(29) That both *financial assistance and the social services for mothers and children should be considerably increased* and should supplement one another, so that, taken together, they would provide for the essential subsistence needs of children.

(30) That the present scheme of *family allowances* should be amended so that the *amount should be raised* to an average allowance of 10*s*.

(31) That the working of the *flat rate benefits* in the present Family Allowances Act should be watched, and if necessary changed, so as to provide higher allowances for older than for younger children, and higher allowances for the third and subsequent children than for the first two.

(32) That *voluntary supplementary schemes* for family allowances in different occupations should be encouraged.

(33) That *benefits for the first child of widows and of unemployed men under the National Insurance Act and of injured men under the Industrial Injuries Act* should be increased.

(34) That *children's rebates under the income tax* should be based on a specific proportion—say 10 per cent—of the total income up to a maximum of a rebate on £150.

(35) That the establishment of *children's rent rebates* should be a statutory obligation on local housing authorities and that a subsidy should be given by these authorities to parents of more than three children in privately owned houses to compensate for any increase in rent of a larger house. Further that *subsidies* should be payable on houses with more than three bedrooms.

(36) That local education authorities should be generous in carrying out the powers given them under the 1944 Education Act for *maintenance grants, bursaries and scholarships* both for schools and universities.

(37) That *subsidies for foodstuffs,* fruit juices, etc., for mothers and children should be retained, as should also the *control of prices and quality* for goods used for children.

(38) That the provisions in the National Insurance Act relating to *mothers' benefits and allowances* should be implemented as soon as possible.

(39) That the *Civil Service and local authorities should pay full salaries* to women in their employ during thirteen weeks' absence for the birth of a child.

(40) That *centres* should be set up by local health authorities to give advice on methods of birth-control; on sterility and sub-fertility; on marriage problems generally; and as to whether any given couple should or should not have children on eugenic grounds. That more *child guidance clinics* should be established.

(41) That the provisions of the National Health Service Act with regard to *services for mothers and children* of all ages should be implemented as soon as possible by all authorities concerned.

(42) That local health authorities should provide *day nurseries* for children from 2 to 5, where the mother is either at work or wishes for relief for a few hours from the care of children; that *children under 2* should only be admitted to the larger nurseries under exceptional circumstances. That, in addition, *small group nurseries* should be organised either by mothers themselves or by voluntary organisations for the care of small groups of children for a few hours each day. That a system of *"sitters-in"* or "home service" women should be organised either by the local health authorities or by voluntary organisations, or by mothers themselves to relieve those who wish for some time off during the day or evening.

(43) That the provisions of the *Education Act 1944* should be carried out as soon as possible to allow (*a*) for more *nursery schools and classes*; (*b*) for *State* schools to be as good as the best of the independent schools with regard to allocation of staff, content of

curriculum, playing fields and other amenities; (*c*) for a rapid extension and improvement of *school meals and school medical service*.

(44) That all forms of *higher education should be provided free* whether at universities, technical colleges or post-university training institutions, students being selected according to their ability.

V. TOWN PLANNING AND HOUSING

(45) That the provision of *desirable surroundings for children* should be a primary object among planning authorities; that these amenities should include open spaces, provision for play, gardens and paddling pools, safety in regard to traffic arrangements and easy access to schools and nurseries.

(46) That in housing schemes a *sufficient number of houses for large families should be provided*. Flats should be limited to four or five stories and should have balconies and lifts; and in all houses bedrooms should be able to be used as bed-sitting rooms.

(47) That *labour-saving devices* connected with heating, lighting, cooking, washing and drying should be provided, and that there should be *adequate provision for prams*.

(48) That the *standard of overcrowding* should be raised to allow for separation of older boys and girls.

VI. STATUS OF MARRIED WOMEN

(49) That public opinion should emphasise that *the bearing and rearing of children* is the finest of all professions for women.

(50) That any legal or customary ban on the *employment of married women* should be removed; and arrangements for *part-time work* be made as far as possible by employers.

(51) That mothers *should not be forced into the labour market* in order to maintain their children.

(52) That the *joint income* of husbands and wives should be divided equally between them.

VII. MIGRATION

Emigration

(53) That once post-war arrangements for men who have served in the war, and wives who have married men from overseas have been carried out, *less encouragement to the emigration of young people of marriageable age or children* should be given.

(54) That *immigration* should be encouraged of *young men and women or children* coming from countries the nationals of which could most easily be assimilated in this country.

(55) That every assistance should be given to these immigrants to learn *the British language and way of life*, that they should be helped and advised and should not be allowed to be exploited. *Naturalisation* should be simpler than at present and immigrants expected to acquire British nationality.

(56) That *pre-war refugees* who are of an age to have children or who can contribute to production should be encouraged to remain.

VIII. QUALITY

(57) That all reforms should be introduced to make it easy for those *parents who are above the average* physically, mentally and morally to have many children.

(58) That *voluntary sterilisation* of those mentally defective, subnormal or diseased should be permitted by law; and that more institutions should be established for those defective persons who do not wish to be sterilised.

BOOK LIST

Abrams, Mark—*The Population of Great Britain.* (George Allen & Unwin. 1945. 3s. 6d.)

Carr-Saunders, A. M.—*World Population.* (Oxford University Press. 1936. 10s. 6d.)

Flügel, J. C.—*Population, Psychology and Peace.* (Watts & Co. 1947. 2s. 6d.)

Glass, D. V.—*Population Policies and Movements.* (Oxford University Press. 1940.)

Glass, D. V., and Blacker, C. P.—*Population and Fertility.* (Population Investigation Committee, 1938. 3s.)

Grundy, Fred, and Titmuss, R. M.—*Report on Luton.* (Leagrave Press, Luton. 1946. 12s. 6d.)

McCleary, G. F.—*The Menace of British Depopulation.* (George Allen & Unwin. 1945. 3s. 6d.)

McCleary, G. F.—*Race Suicide.* (George Allen & Unwin. 1945. 6s.)

Mass Observation—*Britain and Her Birth-rate.* (John Murray. 1945. 21s.)

Marchant, Sir James (Ed.)—*Rebuilding Family Life in the Post-War World.* (Odhams Press. 1945. 2s.)

Myrdal, Alva—*Nation and Family.* (Routledge. 1945. 21s.)

Myrdal, Gunnar—*Population: Today's Question.* (George Allen & Unwin. 1938. 6s.)

Osborn, Frederick—*Preface to Eugenics.* (Harpers. 1940. American.)

Rathbone, Eleanor—*Family Allowances*—a new edition of *The Disinherited Family,* with additional chapters by Lord Beveridge and Eva M. Hubback. (George Allen & Unwin. 1948. 10s. 6d.)

Rathbone, Eleanor—*The Case for Family Allowances.* (Penguin Books. 1940. 9d. Obtainable from the Family Endowment Society.)

Reddaway, W. B.—*The Economics of a Declining Population.* (George Allen & Unwin. 1939. 8s. 6d.)

Scheinfeld, A.—*You and Heredity.* (Chatto & Windus. 1939. 12s. 6d.)

Titmuss, R. M.—*Birth, Poverty and Wealth.* (Hamish Hamilton. 1943. 7s. 6d.)

Titmuss, R. and K.—*Parents' Revolt.* (Secker & Warburg. 1942. 3s. 6d.)

White, Grace Leybourne, and Kenneth White—*Children for Britain.* (Target Series. Pilot Press. 1945. 5s.)

Williams, Gertrude E.—*Women and Work.* (Nicholson & Watson. 1945. 5s.)

PAMPHLETS

Blacker, C. P.—*Eugenics in Prospect and Retrospect.* (Galton Lecture. Hamish Hamilton Medical Books. 1943. 1s. 6d.)

Fabian Society—*Population and the People.* (George Allen & Unwin. 1945. 2s. 6d.)

Harrod, R. F.—*Britain's Future Population.* (Oxford University Press. 1943. 6d.)

Hubback, Eva M.—*Population Facts and Policies.* (George Allen & Unwin. 1945. 2s. 6d.)

Hubback, Eva M.—*A New Plea for Family Allowances.* (Family Endowment Society. 1943. 3d.)

Titmuss, R. M.—*Problems of Population.* (Association for Education in Citizenship. 1943. 4d.)

Workers' Educational Association—*The Future of the Family.* (1944. 3d.)

ORGANISATIONS CONCERNED WITH PROBLEMS OF POPULATION

1. British Social Hygiene Council. (Exhibitions, library, speakers.) Tavistock House, Tavistock Square, W.C.1.

2. Eugenics Society. (Journal, library, speakers.) 69 Eccleston Square, S.W.1.

3. The Family Endowment Society. (Literature, speakers.) 19 Wellgarth Road, N.W.11.

4. Family Planning Association, 69 Eccleston Square, S.W.1.

5. Marriage Guidance Council, 78 Duke Street, W.1.

6. Association for Education in Citizenship, 51 Tothill Street, S.W.1.

NAVIGATION ON THE ROAD?

When the *Queen Mary* enters a busy port, she and all the other vessels obey the recognized lights and signals on which safe navigation depends.

We, too, obey lights and signals — and rely on them for safety — when we drive or ride or walk on the roads.

We are, in fact, "road navigators." Modern traffic simply could not work without a set of rules which we all accept.

Why, then, are there still accidents — far too many?

Partly because we don't all know and understand the rules and principles of Road Navigation. And even if we know them, we forget or ignore them. And partly because some of us don't yet realize that the rules apply to *everyone* — walkers as well as cyclists and drivers. *Any* of us can cause an accident in which we or other people get killed or maimed.

If we all understood the principles of good Road Navigation (based on the Highway Code) and obeyed them *all the time*, traffic would flow faster and more smoothly. We should all get about more easily and, above all, *more safely*. By learning to be skilful Road Navigators, we can help ourselves and everyone else to *get home safe and sound*.

GET HOME SAFE AND SOUND

Issued by the Ministry of Transport

SOME RECENT AND FORTH-COMING BOOKS IN THE PELICAN SERIES